SUDDEN DEATH

STORIES OF A MARINE CORPS RADIOMAN IN THE VIETNAM WAR

GEORGE UHL

STACKPOLE BOOKS

Essex, Connecticut

STACKPOLE BOOKS
The Globe Pequot Publishing Group, Inc.
64 South Main Street
Essex, CT 06426
www.globepequot.com

Copyright © 2025 by George Uhl

All rights reserved. No part of this book may be reproduced in any form or by any electronic or mechanical means, including information storage and retrieval systems, without written permission from the publisher, except by a reviewer who may quote passages in a review.

British Library Cataloguing in Publication Information Available

Library of Congress Cataloging-in-Publication Data Available

ISBN 9780811777629 (cloth) | ISBN 9780811777636 (epub)

*This book is dedicated to the memory of Paul Martin Reed
and all who served during the Vietnam War.
They are our country's cherished sons and daughters who sacrificed
so much for our country. Also, a special thank you to Silver Star recipient
Sergeant William Wright for his courage and selflessness while under fire.*

CONTENTS

Preface		vii
CHAPTER 1	Flashback	1
CHAPTER 2	Gung Ho!	7
CHAPTER 3	Chrome Dome	17
CHAPTER 4	Weekend Warrior	23
CHAPTER 5	"Guerra de Abril" (Dominican Civil War)	33
CHAPTER 6	Curaçao	37
CHAPTER 7	Call to Duty	41
CHAPTER 8	Dead Rats	47
CHAPTER 9	Chuckles	55
CHAPTER 10	Sudden Death	65
CHAPTER 11	Operation Prairie	75
CHAPTER 12	Suzuki	83
CHAPTER 13	Short-Timers	91
CHAPTER 14	No Place Like Home	101
CHAPTER 15	Life Goes On	107
Epilogue		113
Acknowledgments		137
Notes		139

PREFACE

My name is George Uhl, and the stories that you are about to read are a collection of memories based on my military experiences during 1963–1967 while on active duty with the U.S. Marine Corps, focusing on my tour in Vietnam from April 1966–May 1967 to my honorable discharge from Camp Lejeune in August 1967. Over the years I recorded some of the memories and events of my tour in Vietnam, but most were safely stored in the back of my mind like treasured childhood possessions waiting to be freed from confinement.

Writing this book has become a journey that took me back to places long forgotten. Somehow the idea of telling the stories of this young soldier, expressing what I lacked words to convey at the time, came to life and took shape in the form of letters home. The vague memories of experiences in those killing fields of Vietnam have been resurrected and dated to approximate the times of the events.

In December 1963, after basic training on Parris Island (PI), South Carolina, I was stationed at Camp Lejeune, North Carolina. It didn't take long to find out that anyone within driving distance left for home on the weekends, hitching rides with those who had cars. I quickly adapted to the life of a weekend warrior traveling to my family in Pennsylvania.

During those visits, my time was spent relaxing and catching up with high school friends. Invariably, mealtime conversation involved questions about my military activities, allowing me to share my training, duties, and accomplishments. This routine went on for several months until, in 1964, I was deployed overseas for a six-month Mediterranean cruise, followed by a three-month Caribbean cruise. In 1965, I received orders to participate in Operation Power Pack in the Dominican Republic, followed by another cruise to the Caribbean in 1965–1966. During that time, my letters home read like vacation postcards describing the culture, cuisine, and people I met along the way. My last tour of duty was in Vietnam from April 1966 to May 1967. I quickly learned the reality that every day, every hour, and every minute brings fear, constant vigilance, and a flood of emotions as the soldier deals with the trials of war and trying to stay alive.

Combat soldiers have a code of silence. Like the protective instincts of a mother for her child, an unspoken agreement among GIs keeps the brutality of war from the homeland. Letters from the field were rarely graphic, with most soldiers preferring to spare loved ones the anguish of knowing the horrors men and women experience almost daily. The thought of sharing them might expose emotions too raw to deal with in the relative tranquility of normal home life. With a few exceptions, most correspondence described surroundings and pastime activities, complaining about the food and weather, how much we missed our parents, and girlfriends or boyfriends, and home, often ending with requests for cigarettes and cash. To some degree, a parent is not fooled, and I think mine must have really needed the added reassurance of hearing my voice because they sent me a recorder so we could exchange taped conversations. I was grateful to be able to hear their voices. It was then that I realized I could never have told my family the truth about all my experiences during that time in Vietnam, so I decided to fill my letters and tapes with casual news. I still have one or two of those tapes buried in my duffle bag.

Not much has been written about the families of soldiers—the ones anxiously waiting at home, eager for letters and any word confirming that their worst fears have not been realized and that their loved one is okay. Although theirs is not a physical one, they suffer their own mental and emotional war as they adapt to their new normal—waiting and hoping. For couples with one spouse deployed and adjusting their lives to handle the tasks of two people; for families left with the daunting responsibilities of becoming both mother and father; for the families who love, support, and prayed for us while tending to the home fires, this book is for all of you. We owe you so much!

Through research I've discovered much about the Vietnam War that was unknown to me at the time and unseen from a soldier's narrow vantage point from a hooch (tent) or foxhole. Included are also actual letters sent home from Paul Reed, my friend to whom this book is dedicated. At times they are graphic and reveal the truth about his struggles and the anger he felt while in Nam. His letters made it home, but like so many young men who made the ultimate sacrifice, Paul did not.

More than fifty years have passed, and those memories have finally come to life on these pages, revealing what I was unable to share then, fearing the effects on my family. There are many reasons that it has taken so long to give birth to these stories. In some ways, time heals, or at least helps a person come to terms with the past, and after all these years I'm ready to share my experiences before they are lost forever. I know I am one of the lucky ones—to survive my tour in Vietnam and return to my home in one piece. This book is meant to honor those who were less fortunate as well as those who served honorably, and I hope in some way it will help other soldiers who may be dealing with the continued effects caused by the trauma and tragedy of war and often the unacknowledged sacrifices.

God bless our soldiers. We continue to pray for the safe return of our POWs and MIAs and for their families.

FLASHBACK 1

The year was 1985, and nearly two decades had passed since my return from Vietnam in 1967. During the interim years, my first task was to take advantage of the GI Bill to further my education and fulfill my longtime dream of attending art school, which I accomplished when I graduated from the Hussian School of Art in Philadelphia. Shortly after graduation, while employed as a detail draftsman for a design firm, I found a job in sales as a manufacturer's representative, calling on Pittsburgh-area furniture dealers and interior designers. Carol, my future wife, was working as a colorist for one of my accounts, the Pittsburgh Paint Company. I never would have met and asked her out for dinner that day had her boss not requested that Carol keep our appointment in his absence. I began to look forward to my Pittsburgh trips and dinners that led to more dinners as we became aware of our common interests and our attraction for each other grew.

Carol lived in a small apartment on Grand View Avenue that overlooked the city and had a spectacular view of the three rivers (Allegheny, Monongahela, and Ohio). On the quaint tram car that offered commuters a scenic route to and from the city, rides were especially beautiful on moonlit nights with the distant sound of water flowing under twinkling stars. After work, those rides that took us back to her apartment and the magical moments of discovery eventually led to conversations of marriage. One night after dinner at a favorite restaurant, with the warm afterglow of wine filling our senses, I proposed to Carol, and that brief interlude changed the paths of our lives forever.

Our marriage took place in Pittsburgh, officiated by a local justice of the peace, with only Carol's sister and a friend in attendance. We had both been previously married and divorced in the late 1970s. Because we had already experienced the big wedding, the idea of something more intimate and lower key appealed to us. After the JP pronounced us husband and wife, we all gathered near the Three Rivers Stadium where Carol and I shared our personal vows. Ecstatic and eager for new beginnings, we departed Pittsburgh for Rhode Island to share our excitement with Carol's parents, who were traditional, devout Catholics. Apparently new love impairs judgment, and we were not prepared for how deeply we disappointed our parents when we delivered our news. Fortunately, Carol's parents quickly accepted me as their son. Applying some rational thinking, we decided to save money by using the rings from our previous marriages. Carol worked with a local artist she knew for a design, and a jeweler creatively hand-forged them into a unique expression of our commitment to each other.

We soon found new jobs in Philadelphia, said good-bye to Pittsburgh, and moved to Bucks County. Unable to escape my parents' fuss about our elopement, we joyfully celebrated with family and friends and briefly moved in with them until we were able to find our own home in West Chester, a western Pennsylvania suburb. In 1981, I became a dad to our beautiful daughter, Alexis, the delight of our lives. Fatherhood agreed with me, and I doted on her, my heart overflowing with love and wonder at the tiny human being we had conceived. Married life began in earnest, and all we needed was the dog and station wagon, which we quickly added, to complete the picture of the typical happy suburban family.

Four years flew by, and we were living the American dream in beautiful Chester County. Single-mindedly focused on my career as the head of interior design for a large contract furniture dealership, it wasn't unusual for me to work late in my Philadelphia office. I liked working late, craving the peace and quiet after the hectic activity and frantic deadlines. Relishing time alone to complete my day's work, I was able to unwind before my commute home.

After a particularly long day of meetings and paperwork, I was mentally exhausted and depending on the caffeine to give me the energy boost I needed to stay focused so I could finish up and get home. The phones had ceased their incessant ringing, the last employee had departed for the day, and the sounds of street traffic and sirens had faded into relative peace and quiet as the city settled into the dinner hour. Draining the last of my coffee and peering into the dark and dreary night, I gazed past my reflection in the window through the hammering rain into the streets. As I stood watching the drops pounding the glass, listening to the relentless tapping, something about it was familiar.

Memories have a way of creeping into your consciousness. Some grab you by the throat and squeeze until you can't breathe, leaving you terrified and trembling in a heap on the floor, heart pounding and soaking wet from sweat and trying to claw your way back to the present. Some dwell low under the surface and occasionally reappear so you can't shake them off or push them back down into the far recesses of your mind. And some are like annoying gnats that won't be slapped away. Over the years, I had experienced all three types of these persistent memories of a long-ago war. And those were the memories that suddenly clouded out the present as I was transported back to 1966, to my tour of duty in Vietnam.

My military occupational specialty (MOS), the job to which "boots" are assigned, was field radio operator. Along with my personal gear, weapon, ammo, and extra battery, I carried the radio that was our only link to our company for communication, and help if needed. It was up to me to protect it, and I learned to—like a mother bear protects her cubs! Our squad was on a routine search and destroy (S & D) mission to locate, engage, and destroy the enemy, and this was my first time out. We were spread out over a known Viet Cong (VC) trail and set up to ambush or capture "Charlie," which is how we referred to the enemy. Waiting there crouched down in the underbrush alone under the weight of the radio, I listened to the rain making a relentless tapping sound on my poncho. My senses were on high alert, and my heart was beating in anticipation. In addition to the terrifying thoughts of kill or be killed that raced through my mind, we had been warned about the myriad ways the VC used to trap soldiers. Not only were we in danger of encountering the enemy and being ambushed, but the constant threat of booby traps was also everywhere. The training to detect and set booby traps began immediately upon arrival and continued until the day, if we were lucky enough to survive, that we would finally board a transport truck to depart Vietnam for good.

I was becoming drenched and longed for hot coffee and a cigarette. One of the first things you also learned in Nam was not to use any kind of light that Charlie could see that would reveal your position. Lighting a cigarette or smoking was one of many things that could get us killed that night. I guess we were in the rainy season, and under the heavy gray shroud of clouds, it was raining so hard I could only see a few feet ahead. Although I couldn't detect the rest of our squad, I knew they were scattered in the area waiting for the VC to show up. About ten feet off to my right, my buddy John, who was barely a blur, was crouched down, also trying unsuccessfully to keep dry. John and I were both assigned to the 2nd Battalion, 4th Marines, 3rd Marine Division, and quickly became friends. He was an avid Pittsburgh Steelers fan, hailing from Pittsburgh, while I, of course, am a Philadelphia Eagles fan. Because the teams are in different divisions, there was no rivalry between us, and we often spent free time together talking about football, home, and, of course, girls. Peering through the downpour, he smiled at me, and only the white of his teeth was distinguishable under the green and black camouflage paint on his face. We gave each other a thumbs-up and a head nod to indicate that everything was okay. Okay this time!

We got lucky, and our first S & D mission was uneventful, but it could have gone either way, and we knew the reality was that all hell could break loose at any time. Not finding any VC, we stayed just long enough to wait out the rain. We finally made our way back to the command post (CP), which was about an hour's walk, carefully stepping through small streams and rice paddies that were also potentially booby-trapped. I was physically drained and exhausted from the adrenalin and lack of sleep. The sight of our camp on the horizon was a huge relief, though we weren't out of danger yet. Land mines were set up to blast Charlie if he tried to overrun our CP, and we still had to navigate that area before we could safely enter camp. A minefield takes on a whole new meaning when your life is literally at stake!

The mines we used were M18A1 claymore mines that are an anti-infiltration weapon loaded with high explosives (C4) that fires several hundred steel balls about one hundred yards within a sixty-degree arc and operates by remote control. They are pushed into the ground and adjusted by the peep sight to determine the killing zone.[1] Sometimes on a pitch-black night, Charlie would crawl up to the claymores and turn them around, so whenever we heard Charlie and detonated the mines, the load of shot could take out our perimeter of defenses instead. That was only one of many reasons we never got a good night's sleep.

As we approached camp, someone gave the password to the sentry, who confirmed and waved us in. Soaking wet from my boots to my skivvies, I had visions of a hot shower and the warm, dry cot in my hooch. Our camp shower was just another tent beside a four-hundred-gallon mobile tank called a "water buffalo," with a hose hung overhead that supplied a sprayer, but as long as it discharged water, it was good enough for us. There was a waiting line for the shower, so I dried off, stripped down, and crashed onto my cot. It didn't take me long to fall asleep, with my pistol—a .45-caliber handgun—stashed under my pillow and a fragmentation (frag) grenade nearby. Most guys went to bed with their weapons close by for protection against the ever-present danger of VC infiltrating the perimeter. We slept with one eye open and were prepared for anything, making the camp a perilous place for sleepwalkers!

Suddenly my attention returned to the present, and I realized I was in my office, still gazing out the window. I must have been there for at least an hour, lost in a sea of thoughts and overcome with unresolved emotions. I had experienced occasional flashbacks in the past, but this was different—more real. It left me shaking with an anxiety I often felt and generally tried to ignore. It was time to leave, but my memories followed me home, so after dinner I felt compelled to pull out my duffle bag and revisit what I had stowed away for nineteen long years.

Finally, promising myself that I would return to that chapter of my life soon, I repacked the contents safely back into my duffle bag while considering a plan to start writing my stories and possibly having them published someday.

GUNG HO! 2

I was eight years old when my parents, my sister Jean, and I moved to Richboro, one hour north of Philadelphia—a small, one-horse town in Bucks County. Famous for its historic sites, including Washington Crossing Historic Park, the county was founded in 1682 and named Buckinghamshire by William Penn after his family home in England. Although called a suburb, it was typical bucolic America, with acres of cornfields, horses, and country roads, parks, and trails. My dad's dream of owning a home was realized when he purchased a three-quarter-acre lot that backed up to a farm, designed a small ranch-style house, and hired a builder. Compared to our Philadelphia row-house neighborhood with little patches of lawn in the front and sidewalks that met the street, Richboro, with vast areas of green peppered with towering shade trees made for climbing, was a boy's paradise. I often wondered how different my life would have been had we stayed in the city.

The suburbs were tailor-made for carefree adventures. The day we moved into our little house, I met Artie. I happened to glance out my bedroom window and saw him sitting on a donkey in our backyard. He waved. "Hey, kid," he yelled through my bedroom window. "Do you want a ride?" This was something I definitely wouldn't have experienced in our city neighborhood, and he didn't have to ask twice. Artie introduced me to Neil and Mike, and we became lifelong friends. Roaming the fields of Artie's dad's farm on the back of that old donkey, riding his green diesel tractor in the cornfields, riding bikes on country roads, and playing Army were how we spent our summer days.

War games were a favorite for most boys who watched war movies on tiny black-and-white TV screens or in the movies. We played with little green Army men equipped with all of the tactical gear for battles that were enacted in backyards across America. The prized bag of Army soldiers was one of the toys most requested of Santa. Artie's parents' barn, a big weathered red structure that housed their cows, was our shelter and Army command post on rainy days. Two of us would be the enemy and two the brave American soldiers—no one wanted to be the enemy, so we drew straws of hay to decide. Someone would be the officer in charge, whose job it was to fortify our positions against the enemy that we defended with guns made from the never-ending supply of sticks that dropped from the trees at the edge of the property.

My interest in things military actually began at the tender age of five when we lived in Costa Mesa, California. Back-alley battles only required our imagination, pointed fingers for guns, and the noises little boys make to simulate bullets and explosions. One day while playing, after breaching a picket fence to a neighbor's yard, we discovered bags of military uniforms, including helmets and empty cartridge belts. Such a find was too much for our youthful curiosity to pass by, and gleeful shouts of "Wow!" and "Cool!" expressed our excitement. Perhaps the owner was at work, because we browsed and donned the bounty uninterrupted for some time. Much to our delight, someone discovered what looked like bloodstains and a suspicious hole in one of the helmets. After an hour or so, our interest was exhausted, and we returned the contents to the bags and moved on to other adventures. At the time, our young minds couldn't comprehend the significance of what we found. Years later, after the war, when I thought of that experience, I realized we were playing on hallowed ground, with someone's memories finally, it seemed, being laid to rest.

My sisters Joan and Jean were twelve and ten years older than I am. By the time we moved to Richboro, Joan was married and living in Texas with her husband, Earl, who was in the Army. Jean was attending the Philadelphia College of Art and lived with us in Richboro for four years before moving out. My dad was a gentle, patient man who seemed completely unmatched with mom, who had a quick temper. He was an electrical engineer who worked at the shipyard in Philadelphia for a local engineering firm and came home late every night. My mother was a housewife, and I guess I never gave a second thought to the cleaning, cooking, and laundry she constantly did for us, as well as managing the house in Dad's absence. She was a strict, nononsense disciplinarian who could be very tough at times, especially with my sisters. Although I was pretty quiet around the house and played outside most of the time, I learned early when to stay out of Mom's way.

Mom and Jean rarely saw eye to eye on anything, especially on Jean's boyfriends. For some reason, Mom didn't seem to like any of them, so Mom and Jean argued constantly. I just added to Jean's misery by being a constant tease. Usually I was banished to my bedroom or outside before her dates arrived, with strict orders to "Stay out of the way!" One day while Jean was at school, I was practicing tricks with my new all-wood Duncan yo-yo and had a brainstorm. Thinking how cool it would be if my yo-yo sparkled, it occurred to me that rhinestones would be an awesome embellishment—I knew exactly where to find what I needed. In the contents of Jean's jewelry box was the perfect solution! Gathering a handful of trinkets that I thought she might not miss, I commenced prying them from their settings and gluing on the dazzling little stones until both sides of the yo-yo were covered. Admiring my handiwork, I set out to show off my creation to my buddies, proudly executing a dazzling "around the world" trick that elicited admiring comments and was well worth the wrath of Jean, which I was sure to provoke. Tired from school and her commute, Jean sought the refuge of her spotless bedroom when she arrived home, only to discover her jewelry box in an unaccustomed state of disorder and some gems missing. I was safely hidden in my bedroom with my chair against the door when I heard her scream, "Geeooorrge!!" and my startled mother yelling from the kitchen, "What happened?!" I did not show my face again until, having missed my afternoon snack, I was hungry enough to brave the dinner table and my irate sister, who slapped the back of my head and threatened to kill me if I ever entered her room again.

With the distance in our ages, Jean and I never had the chance to be close when we were young, but I always looked up to her. She was a talented artist who made a successful career as a painter, traveled the world offering workshops, and published an acclaimed book on watercoloring. Jean and husband Ron, a well-known artist and sculptor, are parents to Scott, also an artist, and Jeff, who is a musician, and also grandparents to four grandchildren. In high school I was a fair student, but what really interested me was art, especially the field trips that gave me the opportunity to sketch nature and the surrounding farmlands I loved. I didn't know it then, but Jean had a definite influence on me. I think I always wanted to follow in her footsteps, and in later years art would be my passion, and in a way part of my future careers.

In those days, most kids joined the Scouts. I joined the Cub Scouts and later the Boy Scouts. Dad, an Eagle Scout, was our scoutmaster and mentor. Becoming an Eagle Scout, the highest rank attainable in the Scouts program, which requires at least twenty-one merit badges, is achieved by only 4 percent of Scouts. Dad took us on weekend camping trips where we'd hike and canoe along the Delaware Canal and set up tents on the mule path. We had no idea of its amazing history. Renamed the Delaware Canal State Park in 1989, the canal, which runs sixty miles parallel to the right bank of the Delaware River, is preserved today as the last towpath canal in America capable of being fully watered and restored.

The mornings were frigid and damp, and our day started early. Resisting Dad's unwelcome wake-up calls, we'd burrow into our sleeping bags, unwilling to leave our warm nests until shrill whistle calls and rumbling stomachs lured us out to make breakfast and break camp. I have to give him credit for the way he expertly managed nine twelve-year-old boys while supervising the morning activities. The sounds of nature, the surging of the river rapids, and the smell of pancakes cooking on the fire are vivid and wonderful memories that I often revisit fondly, having experienced it with my dad. Much later, I would remember how kind and humble he was, qualities that made him an exceptional person, and I hoped that I would measure up in some way. I didn't make it to Eagle Scout but earned Life Scout, which is just below the Eagle Scout badge. Later on, I became an Explorer Scout. I now understand how Scout training helped me all through life with discipline and readiness and, I guess in a way, with my first military experience.

My high school was located next to a farm where "fragrances" were in abundance! Early every morning during spring, the fields were spread with manure. Our school windows were opened, and the cool breeze blew into our classrooms with the pungent aroma wafting through, clearing our senses and watering our eyes!

Football was the pastime of choice, and I joined junior varsity in my sophomore year. After my second year, I realized I'd never make varsity. One afternoon while watching the track team running a 440 (one lap around the track), I decided to ask the coach if I could try out. I was a skinny kid with long legs, lots of energy, and a history of racing around fields and farmland with my friends for hours. Coach said go ahead, and I ran like hell and beat everyone to the finish line. He walked over, patted me on the back, and said I could switch to track and field. I lettered in my senior year and earned a coveted letterman's sweater, which was a big deal. I wore mine proudly, especially around the girls!

With $25 that I borrowed from my dad, I bought my first car from a senior in high school who was going into the Army. It was a 1952 pea-green Studebaker with fabric seats and overdrive, and you couldn't tell if it was coming or going because the front and back looked almost the same. I instantly gained my freedom and lots of new friends. When I was not with my buddies, I would drive to the other end of Bucks County to visit my sister Joan who had moved back from Texas and settled in Levittown. By then, Joan and Earl had three little boys named Jim, Tim, and Kim, who became my pals. Joan and Earl's house became a regular hangout, and I often showed up unannounced looking for some rambunctious fun and a meal. Their house was small, comfortable, and welcoming, with a sliding door off the dining room that opened to a cement patio. Next to it stood a well-used grill that produced hotdogs nonstop and a table with thirst-quenching lemonade. The yard was scattered with lawn chairs, water toys, and balls of all sorts, and the back corner housed a shiny aqua vinyl aboveground pool big enough to allow three boys and a teenager plenty of room for hours of roughhousing. I loved playing with the boys, who looked up to their older cousin, and I had no trouble convincing them that I was "The All Great and Powerful Uncle George," a title that has stuck to this day.

It was 1963, and I was in my senior year of high school. I was more than ready for graduation and my independence, but that did not diminish the bittersweet feelings of leaving behind childhood friends and my first love. I had seen Lynn with Jim, one of my classmates around school, and knew they had been a couple for a while. When they broke up at our friend's birthday party and he left with his new attraction, Candy, I noticed Lynn standing alone in a corner, so I wandered over and asked her to dance. Lynn was petite with curves in the right places and pretty eyes that lit up when she laughed. Glancing around the room filled with couples "making out," I found us a place to sit. We talked for a while, and I wondered what it would be like to kiss her. I hoped she couldn't hear my heart pounding as I placed my arm around the back of the sofa. Deciding to take a chance, I casually draped it over her shoulder and caressed her arm as we sat talking. As she settled closer and looked up at me, I gently reached down and brushed her soft lips with mine. Looking into my eyes, she returned my kiss, and I pulled her closer. We spent the rest of the evening locked in each other's arms, and from that night on we were inseparable.

Walking arm in arm into our favorite hangouts and around school between classes, we became known as a couple and settled into a comfortable pattern of meeting before the first bell, sharing lunch, and talking on the phone. Friday nights and weekends were filled with plans to look forward to, but I must have missed any signs that our relationship changed. Lynn and her mom went to Virginia to visit family for a week over the Christmas holiday. Unaccustomed to being alone, I found myself floundering with extra time and yearning for the week to end so we could return to school and our familiar routine. The day they returned, I immediately phoned her, but my calls went unanswered. In school she avoided me and made excuses of obligations. Finally, one of her friends broke it to me that she was dating someone else. I was devastated and angry to find out through a friend. Breaking up, as they say, is so very hard to do, and my heart was broken.

Dreading every encounter with her, I found myself avoiding my usual routes through the halls to class and avoided familiar hangouts where they might be together. I went to the senior prom alone and stood with the guys with no dates. Stealing glances at her and wishing she was back in my arms,

I could almost smell her perfume and feel her soft body against mine. Unable to suppress my desire for her and afraid it would show, I walked out to join the others for a smoke. As they played the last dance, I collected my buddies to get a bite to eat. I wanted to be gone before the crowd started to leave, knowing cars would fill with couples shouting confirmations of post-prom celebrating. The following week until graduation day was just a blur of disappointment with me feeling sorry for myself.

I had always thought about the military for a career and was torn between that and art school. My uncle was in the Air Force and was always traveling somewhere. During homecomings, he regaled us with stories of his adventures, which sounded pretty exciting to a teenager hoping to break away from family, so the thought of being a soldier like my uncle lingered in the back of my mind. I also heard about Grandpa Frank, my dad's father, who built small trucks out of scrap parts in his garage and gave them to the military for the war effort during World War II. He had some kind of physical issues that prevented him from serving, but like most people then, he wanted to contribute in any way he could.

Every boy loved to watch war movies with gripping tales of heroism, and they were probably the best recruitment vehicles the military could have devised when they enlisted the help of the entertainment industry for World War II. All of this probably impacted and contributed to my desire to know more about the military. Finally, one day, without mentioning it to anyone, I took a drive into Philadelphia and visited all the recruiting offices. My first stop was the Navy recruitment center. I walked out after a short discussion that left me feeling unmotivated. The Air Force recruiter tried to talk me into enlisting but had no guarantees for an assignment, so I decided to try the Marines who, to me, seemed to be synonymous with strength and bravery. The walls of all the recruiting offices were lined with huge posters designed to entice young men with words of excellence and bravery. There on the walls, I saw the words that convinced me—the few, the strong, and the brave—and I knew it was for me.

As the recruiter brought me coffee and reassured me that this was the right decision, I found myself taking the test and signing the papers. It was impulsive, and I really hadn't realized the magnitude of what I'd done until, on hearing the news, my totally distraught mother demanded that my dad take me back to the center to "un-sign" the papers. It took a while, but Dad and I managed to calm her down, and I convinced them that I knew what I was doing, at least we hoped. This was the first time I had stood up to my parents and taken charge of my life, so in my mind I was ready. It was a done deal, but little did I know what lay ahead. In the blink of an eye, I graduated from high school, and my enlistment was looming over my head. I only had a few months left before I would be off to Parris Island, South Carolina, but first I was looking forward to some shore time.

Every year my parents rented a summer home in Ocean City, New Jersey, for a week or two. Both of my sisters stayed all summer—Jean at Flanders Hotel and Joan at a boarding house as they worked to earn money for college. Dad arrived Friday evenings for the weekend and returned to work on Mondays, leaving me with Mom, who occasionally came to the beach, but mostly she just stayed at the shore house and did what she did at home. I was free to spend my days swimming and hanging out with friends without a care in the world and only thoughts of how to fill my days with sun and fun. It would be years before I realized how fortunate and idyllic my youth had been, with no concept that others lived less charmed lives. Looking back, I realize I didn't see much of Mom then and didn't give much thought to her life except how it affected me. Later, during my military years, I began to wish there had been a deeper connection and tried to make it up to her, especially after our daughter Alexis was born.

By the time I graduated from high school, my sisters were out of college and working, and my parents didn't come to the shore that summer. It would be my last year at Ocean City for a long time and my first alone without my family. But I didn't mind—I was looking forward to being on my own. Summer at the shore for a teenager was like nothing else in the world, staying up late hanging out and sleeping all morning. Over the years I had made friends that I looked forward to seeing. Our crowd met at the College Grill on 14th Street where we occupied booths and passed carefree hours drinking cherry Cokes or hanging out on the boardwalk eating boardwalk fries with vinegar.

I immediately found a job working evenings until closing at Frank's Arcade House on the boardwalk, where I gave change to customers to play the games. I could meet a lot of girls and get paid, which wasn't a bad deal. Though not much money, in those days you could live on pocket change, and all I needed was enough to pay room rent, gas, and food. Considering you could get lunch for $1.50, dinner for $2.00, and gas for 25¢ a gallon, plus I rarely drove on or off the island, I even managed to save money.

Working the evening shift gave me the entire day to myself, but the best part of the day happened after work when our gang got back together at the boardwalk pavilion. We passed the night strumming our guitars and singing oldies off-key, our youthful voices declaring our innermost thoughts and passions.

The music hall where we hung out and danced was at the north end of the boardwalk overlooking the ocean. Vast doors were left open to let the sea breeze in. Live or recorded music intruded into the peaceful evenings, and pretty girls with tanned bodies and swinging hips entertained eager boys with a variety of dance moves. Lining the walls were the onlookers, who alternately cut in or watched from the sidelines, imagining themselves gently swaying to the heady music in the arms of any one of the pretty young females gracing the hall. I was one of the lucky guys who found a steady. I had seen Karen several times at the arcade where I worked, and one night I mustered up the courage to ask her out. After I finished work, we would meet at the music hall and hang out with friends until the heat and rising passion from slow dancing drove us outside to the ramp that led under the boardwalk. Make-out sessions ended with cool walks on the beach and finally to her parents' house, where we parted with our last kiss of the evening.

One night a guy came up to me and asked if I wanted a small bottle of wine for a dollar. Occasionally, back home, my friends and I secretly had a few beers that we got from someone's house, but I never got drunk or in trouble and wasn't prepared for how my dollar bottle of wine would affect me. Someone said to mix it with soda to cut the alcohol, which made it taste like a soft drink and go down real easy.

I don't remember much about that night, but the next day I woke up in the backseat of my car parked in an alley, covered in wet sand, and smelling like puke. I had no idea how I got there or what had happened, but I got cleaned up, drove to my friend's house, and softly knocked on the door, hoping not to encounter his parents. He opened the door, turned white, and said he thought I was dead. I answered, "No, I am alive, barely, but I'm not sure what happened to me." So we sat down on the step, and he told me a crazy story of my night's misadventure. The wine was a homemade mixture of Thunderbird wine and grain alcohol. He said I was acting weird at the dance hall and mumbling my words. They tried to get me to sleep it off, but when they left me alone, I got up and staggered down the boardwalk and made my way to the College Grill. Later I remembered climbing on a stool and slurring something about ordering breakfast, but they wouldn't serve me, so I decided to take a swim.

It was a miracle I didn't drown, and I didn't remember that it took three or four kids to get me out of the water and back to the boardwalk while I apparently cursed and fought them all the way. A police officer who recognized me came to my rescue. He helped find my car, threw me in, and drove it to an alley behind my apartment so I could sleep it off. Most of the local police knew us and were probably used to handling the antics of the summer kids. That night could have gone very differently, and I knew I lucked out!

The rest of the summer passed by quickly, and soon it was August. Before I knew it, I was heading home to pack and prepare for boot camp. After saying my good-byes to my family and friends and breaking free of the tearful death grip of my mother, who was inconsolable, my father drove me to the recruiting center in Philadelphia. It was harder leaving home than I expected, but I was all gung ho and just looking forward to my future. For the first time in my life, I was in control, free to make my own decisions—or so I thought—and it felt good. As I opened the door, Dad grabbed my arm, looked me squarely in the eyes, and said, "Keep your mouth shut, do what they tell you, and make us proud."

I was a little scared and nervous, and as I walked into the old brick recruiting center at the naval base, I noticed there were about twenty other sorry-looking recruits in the room looking equally nervous. Joking around a little and trying to be cool, we did not have much time to get to know each other before the officer in charge barked out a call to attention, a command I understood from the Boy Scouts, and we all jumped into place. Instructions to perform a series of exercises quickly weeded out several of the recruits who were asked to leave. I was in fairly good shape and had endurance from swimming, so I managed the required pull-ups. After that, we were sworn in and bused to the train station. We were on our way to Parris Island (PI), and life as I knew it was about to change!

CHROME DOME 3

After our swearing in at the recruitment center in Philadelphia, the realization set in that I was officially a Marine recruit and that there would be no turning back. We boarded the train and made our way through the cars, found our not-so-comfortable stained fabric seats, and settled in for the trip to PI. I noticed that the car was eerily quiet except for the whistle and loud clatter of the train wheels as we pulled away from the station. Not a word was uttered from what would normally be a talkative, if not rowdy, car full of young men. The conductor must have been through this many times and correctly assumed we were new recruits bound for PI. As he punched our tickets, he stopped for a minute and, looking us over, said, "Good luck. You will need it!"

I guess we were all thinking the same thing—what have we gotten ourselves into and what lies ahead for us? I don't remember being scared, but I was tired and edgy. As the train picked up speed, we began to relax and introduced ourselves to each other, sharing stories about home and families to pass the time. At some point we all fell asleep, only to be awakened by the conductor announcing that we had arrived. I remember stepping off the train and into the stifling South Carolina August heat that momentarily took my breath away. This was quite different from the northern summer heat I was accustomed to, and I found myself imagining something tall, cold, and wet to drink. Instead, we were immediately greeted by a Marine sergeant whose first words were "Shut up, and don't speak unless spoken to!" Then he barked out an order for us to get on the bus that would take us to PI.

Dear Mom and Dad,   *8/25/63*
We arrived at PI (Parris Island) on August 20th, and I was assigned to Platoon 366, 2nd Recruit Battalion. Our first stop on base was the receiving barracks, and I made the big mistake of getting off the bus first. We were greeted by a Marine sergeant, and

this guy was REALLY HUGE. *His uniform was spotless, the brass buckle on his belt shone in the sunlight, you could see your reflection in his polished boots, and he had a Real. Bad. Attitude. He looked at me and bellowed, "Pick up that trash on the ground, Private, and put it in a dipsy dumpster." I had no clue what a dipsy dumpster was, so I asked, "Can you please tell me what a dipsy dumpster is?" He looked at me like I was lunch and bellowed again, "DO NOT CALL ME EWE. A EWE IS A SHEEP, NOT YOUR SERGEANT." I grabbed the trash, found the dumpster, and waited for his next command, just happy to be alive. We finally arrived at our barracks and were greeted by our drill instructors (DIs) where they lined us up into formation and lost no time getting in our faces. After thoroughly insulting and demeaning everyone, they marched us in the heat to a building and told us to strip down to our dog tags. We were given bags for our clothes and personal stuff including our wallets, which they said would be returned after boot camp. We were issued uniforms and our "783 gear"—basically all of our equipment in a bucket—and rifles. The worst thing for everyone was the "boot camp skinhead" haircuts, and for the guys who needed them, gross, black-framed military glasses.*

There are lots of rules. Our DI makes us enter the mess hall in order and leave in the same order, and based on our physical size, we are told how much to eat. This is great for me since I weighed in at 135 lbs. I can eat as much as I want, and I think I've gained 10 lbs. But I really feel sorry for the guys that are heavy. They have to lose weight fast, and if they don't, they can be sent to a rehab squad that specializes in weight loss. Of those sent, only a few have returned to rejoin our platoon.

Have to go for now. Do not worry—I'm hanging in there, and I'll write again soon. Love, George

Several platoons are in training at the same time. There are seventy-five men in the average Marine recruit platoon. From the moment a platoon is formed, it's clear that the goal is to be the best, and the DIs are relentless in their expectations as they train and drill their recruits. This constant drilling is used to develop teamwork and to teach instant obedience to commands. Marching in formation becomes a way of life and is employed throughout the day wherever recruits travel on base. Day and overnight marches they call preparedness for war start at five miles, increasing to twenty-five miles, with full gear, weighing as much as forty pounds. There is no advanced warning of these marches or the "confidence courses"—obstacle courses that push the recruit's physical abilities to the limit in the hot South Carolina sun, which can be unbearable most days, and there is always a danger of heat exhaustion. When conditions are too hot for marching and drilling, a black flag is run halfway up the flagpole. We weren't sure whose idea it was, but the recruits might have disagreed with their definition of hot.

For the first six to eight weeks in boot camp, recruits can't smoke, talk, or relax. The DIs called us "chrome domes" because we wore helmets that looked like shiny metal and were hot. They also referred to us as whale shit and dogged us 24/7. The military owned us, and we had no freedom or rights. Marine recruits come from diverse backgrounds, so it is important to have one set of rules. It takes twelve weeks to go through the process, and during that time, those who cannot keep up are weeded out. I was starting to get the picture. We were being molded and transformed into highly disciplined "green machines." The plan was to tear you down physically and mentally and rebuild you. If you survived, you became a Marine. When you graduated boot camp, there was a sense of accomplishment and brotherhood that would stay with you for life.

> Dear Mom and Dad, 9/15/63
> Yesterday, our platoon was grouped in the squad bay (sleeping quarters) and instructed to sit on the floor. The DI was barking out a lecture when suddenly he stopped and shouted, "I want all the niggers to stand up now!" We have four black guys in our platoon. Three immediately obeyed the order and stood up, and the fourth didn't. We were wondering what would happen next when the DI said, "I want all of you to look at this man who did not stand. He has pride in himself, and even at the risk of disobeying my order, he did not allow himself to be degraded. That belief best represents the pride of the Marine Corps." That was a lesson to us about pride and respect in ourselves. The military is full of surprises! It's been a long day, and I'm looking forward to some shut-eye. Hope you are well. Looking forward to your next letter.
> Love, George
> P.S. Dad, how is my car running?

Midway through training, my parents showed up without telling me. We were all in the squad bay when the DI bellowed in front of the entire platoon that my parents were outside waiting to see me. Great! Surprised and slightly embarrassed, I walked out as though this was a daily occurrence, trying to act nonchalant amid whistles and pokes and shouts of "Hey, Uhl, Mommy and Daddy are here to see you!" But when I saw them standing by the car, I realized how much I missed them and how glad I was that they came. South Carolina from Philadelphia is a really long trip for a short visit, and I felt like they brought a piece of home with them. The fact that they brought me candy, soda, and cigarettes did not hurt either.

Unable to break free of my mother's bear hug as she tearfully asked if I was okay, I did my best to reassure her that I was fine. Dad didn't say much, and I could see he was trying to control his emotions as he firmly shook my hand and slapped my back. Curious about the base and all that was happening around us, they alternately fired questions at me. With no place available to receive guests, we sat in the hot car with the South Carolina sun pouring through the windows. Minutes ticked away as I attempted to explain the buildings and layout of our sprawling base while stuffing my mouth with the candy they brought and downing sodas in an attempt to stay cool. At one point I noticed Mom watching me intently, her normally stern look softened, and I felt that perhaps she was no longer angry and maybe even a little proud of me. That hour flew by, and saying good-bye was harder than I expected as they drove off into the night.

Dear Mom and Dad, 10/8/63
I was really surprised when you showed up on base. I know I said this already, but I guess I didn't realize how much I missed you. Thanks for taking the time to drive all that way. I hope the ride was not tiring and you got in the golf you were planning. Where did you play?

Not much new happening except I had a little accident. We were in the squad bay at attention, and the DI gave us an order to double-time to the showers. We all ran as fast as we could, but unfortunately someone left a metal scrub bucket in the way. I hit it with my foot at full speed and sliced open my right toe. I was dripping blood everywhere, and the DI barked at someone to hand me a band-aid. I can still get into my boots, but it hasn't been easy to keep up with training, especially marching. Amazing how a little toe can make life so miserable. I can't imagine getting shot! Don't worry, I'm fine, but I can tell you I'm real glad to get my feet out of those boots at the end of the day!

We were tested for our job assignments. I really wanted to be a radio operator and hoped my Scout training would get me through Morse code. I tried the best I could, but I didn't pass the test. I was assigned to be a 2511 (job number for wireman). When I get to Camp Lejeune, I will start training, but right now we're all just really looking forward to graduating.

Glad you got a new riding lawn mower. Wish we had that when I was cutting the grass!!
Love, George

Dear Mom and Dad, 10/25/63
Yesterday our platoon sergeant marched us to an area that had several small metal-roof huts that smelled really bad. We were told this would be our chemical warfare training. I doubt if any of us ever thought about chemical warfare, and at that point we all probably looked at him like deer in headlights. As we walked into the hut, they handed each of us a gas mask and instructed us how to use it in the event of gas exposure. Suddenly without warning (to simulate a real attack) the room filled with gas, and we all started coughing and choking. Our eyes were watering and burning so badly we couldn't see, and it got worse when we rubbed them. Holding our breath, we struggled to get our masks on as fast as we could, and one guy was having so much trouble breathing they took him outside. We stayed in the room for about 10 minutes until the instructor told us to take off our masks. Finally, we were guided out of the hut, and I have never appreciated fresh air so much! We only received a small amount of gas, and the

entire exercise was monitored very closely, but it took about 30 minutes to get my lungs clear and back to normal breathing. If that was not bad enough, the instructor handed out counter chemical warfare syringes and told us to stick our thighs and squeeze in the agent, which is supposed to neutralize the gas. You know how much I hate needles, and I really had a hard time sticking myself, but we all had to do it because in battle you have no choice if you want to live. I know the instructor was watching over everyone closely, so we were never in any real danger, but it's an exercise I'll never forget and never want to repeat. Ironically today they gave us permission to smoke cigarettes in the smoking circle outside of our barracks. Gassed one day and smoking the next! It really hurt my lungs taking that first drag, but I managed to get over it.

That is about it for now. How are Joan and Jean and the boys doing? Please say hi for me. Can't wait to see you at my graduation ceremonies. Not everyone's family can make it, and it means a lot to me that you will be here.
Love, George

It had been a long twelve weeks, and the final three weeks prior to graduation day were spent in preparation for the ceremony. Evening activities were shining brass, "spit shining" our shoes, and cleaning our M14 rifles under the eagle eyes of the drill instructors; nothing less than perfection was demanded.

Graduation is the day recruits are addressed as "Marines" for the first time. On that morning of November 17, 1963, we cleaned our rifles and rechecked our uniforms. After final words from our DI to reassure and prepare us, we assembled outside and joined the other platoons for a final inspection of each recruit by the officer in charge. We then marched to the parade grounds for the final "pass and review" (the march past the camp commander and spectators). The actual ceremony is carried out with precision timing—each soldier with a 30" spread to his stride in perfect step and performing parade maneuvers to the commands of the drill sergeant. I knew my parents were somewhere in the stands among the spectators, struggling to recognize me among the rows of dress greens and no doubt bursting with pride.

After the ceremony, the drill instructors (no longer addressed as "sir"—that title now reserved for officers) shook our hands and congratulated us individually. Our twelve weeks of boot camp training had officially ended. We had gotten off the bus as a cocky ragtag group of guys and left the parade grounds as Marines. I finally located my parents among the sea of visitors. Handing them my certificate of graduation, I stepped into my teary-eyed mom's familiar bear hug and shook hands with my dad who was smiling ear to ear as he affectionately slapped me on the back as they kept telling me how proud they were. It took them twelve hours to get here, and in two hours it was all over, and I was saying good-bye again. I started missing them the minute they left.

We all thought we were done and ready to start work in our assigned fields, but instead we were told that we had to go to infantry training (IT) for three to four more weeks in North Carolina. Three more weeks of training in the field were not expected, but after three months at PI, we could manage to do three more weeks. Infantry training consisted of field tactics with simulated combat conditions. We got on a bus and arrived for IT at Camp Geiger located in the woods south of Camp Lejeune, North Carolina, near New River, on November 18, 1963.

The tragic assassination of President Kennedy occurred four days after our arrival, and with no access to news, we heard only that the president had been shot and died shortly after. It would be a few weeks before we had actual details, including the tragedy of what the First Lady had undergone and the swearing in of Vice President Johnson on Air Force One en route back to Washington, DC. By then the president's funeral on November 25 had taken place. The crowds watched his tiny son John, surrounded by the Kennedy family, as he saluted the passing casket taking his father to his final resting place in Arlington National Cemetery. The funeral took all day and ended with the soldiers firing a three-gun salute and a bugler playing "The Last Post." Mrs. Kennedy and Bobby Kennedy lit the eternal flame at the president's temporary grave. Later, the John F. Kennedy Eternal Flame, designed by John Carl Warnecke, a longtime personal friend of the president, became the permanent site.[1]

Dear Mom and Dad,   *11/22/63*
We're in our first week of infantry training at Camp Geiger out in the woods. Today class was interrupted when another instructor pulled aside the sergeant. Staring down at the ground for a minute before looking at each of us, he hesitated, then told us President Kennedy had been shot in Dallas, Texas. Our mouths were all open in shock, and we stood there in silence trying to absorb the unbelievable news. After a short break, the sergeant offered a prayer for the president and his family. Later we got word that the president died, and we were sent back to our barracks. We do not have access to news out here, and we haven't heard anything about the president's family or the funeral, but I'm sure it's all over the evening news and papers at home. I just don't know what to say or think, and I'm sure the entire country feels the same. Everyone here is so quiet, and we have not really discussed the assassination, but I think we were all feeling really angry and shocked that this could happen in America.

I keep thinking of how all of you are taking it at home. I remember the quote from President Kennedy's speech, "Ask not what your country can do for you, ask what you can do for your country,"[2] and I feel like serving in the military is something I can do, especially when our commander-in-chief gave his life for his country.

In a few weeks I will be at Camp Lejeune. Please write and let me know everything that is going on and how everyone is doing.
Love, George

WEEKEND WARRIOR 4

After completing infantry training, I was stationed at Camp Lejeune with the 3rd Battalion, 10th Marines, 2nd Marine Division, and reported for duty on December 17, 1963. I was ecstatic to learn they had given me a five-day-leave pass starting on December 21, which meant I'd be home for Christmas, and they didn't have to tell me twice! As I started packing and filling out the leave forms, I realized that I had to find a way to get home. The sergeant in charge informed me that for $15–$20 round-trip, you could always find a ride with a "weekend warrior." Everyone was anxious to get home as often as possible, and it didn't matter with whom or how many were loaded into a car as long as it was going our way. I got a ride with a guy who had a hot two-door '55 Chevy. He was willing to take my cash and cram one more into his car, and we left for Pennsylvania that day at noon.

Time slipped away with the miles as we passed through familiar towns drawing closer to home, and I felt myself contemplating how to spend the next five glorious days of freedom. Home meant sleeping in my bed, home-cooked meals, meeting high school friends at our old hangout, eating my favorite fries and drinking cherry Coke, and catching up with my buddies. I felt like I had been away forever and could not wait to see everyone.

When we arrived in Philadelphia late that night, my dad was waiting for me. I thanked the guys for the ride and packed my gear into Dad's car for the last leg of my journey home to my anxiously waiting mother and all of my family. Sitting around the dining-room table, each of us in our usual chair, I settled back into our comfortable home life as they filled me in on family and community events. The drive and excitement of coming back for the first time caught up with me quickly, and I soon said good night and happily crashed on the familiar old lumpy mattress in my room surrounded by my childhood possessions. The only thing on my mind the next morning was meeting up with my old friends, most of whom had entered college and were also home for the holidays. It was over soda and fries that I discovered that my ex-girlfriend Lynn was dating someone. Thinking back for a moment on those last weeks of high school, I felt the old sting of hurt and disappointment, but that soon passed. The rest of my visit was spent showing off the new 1962 Nash Rambler my dad had bought me after the old Studebaker had a fatal engine problem, and filling the guys in about the rigors of boot camp. That was the first of many weekend trips home whenever I was on base and the pattern of my life for the next two years.

Before I knew it, I was saying my good-byes and savoring that last hour with Dad as he drove me to the pickup place in Philadelphia. As we arrived at dusk, the '55 Chevy was waiting with the engine running and a load of Marines ready for the long drive back to Camp Lejeune. I waved good-bye to Dad and squeezed into the backseat. During the next eight hours, we took turns driving and sleeping. I remember driving the last few hours with everyone in the car asleep, counting on me to get them back safely. As night closed in, the monotony of the drive began to lull me from boredom to drowsiness. My eyes became lead, and my head periodically drooped and snapped back as I struggled to pay attention to the traffic and stay on the road. I was about ready to pull over when the sun appeared on the horizon, rising up to its full splendor, and the bright light woke me up. I managed to stay alert until we arrived at the base just on time to make morning formation. Every morning on base begins with formation and roll call, and not appearing is considered unauthorized absence (UA). This is a serious offense and can result in the penalty of a reduction in rank, loss of pay, or the extreme: time in the brig (military prison). Such offenses are noted in the United States Military Code of Conduct.

Dear Mom and Dad,   *12/30/63*
As I mentioned when I was home, I've been assigned to a communication company as a wireman. I was hoping to have formal military school training but was assigned on-the-job training (OJT) instead. Classes have just begun, and the corporal who is instructing us is patient and takes the time to explain the job details and answer our questions. Unlike the DIs, he isn't constantly yelling at us, and it's a lot less stressful!

We are learning to install EE-8 field telephones to SB-22 switchboards. I started out running ground lines and installing equipment. That was fine until we had to climb trees to run the telephone lines. I am somewhat okay with the heights, but it was a bit unnerving to hear we'd be asked to climb a 30–40' pole. The corporal explained the process and safety precautions. You first strap a leg harness, which has a spike next to your inner foot, to each leg. We wear a large belt that has a hook for a harness that wraps around the pole. Then you climb by raising the belt up the pole while sticking the spikes in the pole as you climb. I climbed the pole, and when I reached the top the corporal said, "Here, catch this!" as he threw a football at me. I instinctively reached out and caught the ball before realizing what happened as I stood on the spike in shock! He said that it was a confidence test and that I passed. I am now an official wireman.

Yesterday our entire company went on an operation for a field training exercise where we are taught on telephone poles, but in the actual field where there are no poles, we will be climbing and wiring trees. Where there are no trees, we lay ground lines, otherwise known as landlines. Our destination was a few hours away, and as our convoy passed mile after mile of poles, I realized that it never occurred to me I would have a job running telephone lines. Life is funny. I also never gave a thought as to what it takes to make a simple phone call. Now here I am, shimmying up poles that provide the service to keep open the lifelines of communication.

Most of our time is spent cleaning EE8 field telephones and other World War II equipment. We are going on several amphibious training exercises on the beaches of South Carolina, and I am becoming proficient at running lines and operating the telephone switchboard. I really wanted to be a field radio operator and requested training, but I was told I would have to do it on my own time, which I'm doing, and will be able to change my MOS (military occupational specialty) by the end of my second year.

I need to go now,
Love, George

The main responsibility of the field radio operator is to provide a communication link between the infantry and the command post (CP). Another important responsibility is to help the officer in charge communicate with his superior officer and to spot enemy positions, call in the coordinates, and coordinate the firing of various artillery to eliminate or destroy the target. When the enemy is spotted from a forward position, a "fire mission" is radioed back to the CP, which directs the mission to the artillery command (air, naval, or tank) to start the mission by ordering smoke rounds. Smoke rounds are used to pinpoint the enemy positions. These rounds are fired and adjusted close to the enemy before ordering high-explosive (HE) rounds to the target on the command "fire HE for effect."

In January 1964, I signed up for a Mediterranean cruise. Our fleet was stationed in the Med for support of our allies and Americans. We practiced mock landings in Spain and other countries to keep our troops and equipment ready. The best thing about the cruise was having liberty in all the ports in the Mediterranean. I was fortunate to see Spain, Italy, and Greece. Our first stop was Spain where we conducted landing exercises, after which we were given liberty in Barcelona.

Dear Mom and Dad,   1/5/64
Our company formed together at the Navy base in Norfolk, Virginia, to embark for a Mediterranean cruise. Our ship was a landing platform dock (LPD), primarily used for landing Marines, their equipment, supplies, landing craft, and helicopters. Finding

my bunk was a nightmare. I finally located it somewhere midship at the lowest level. I knew some of the guys from my company, but we had a few new faces joining our team. We introduced ourselves to the new guys and wasted no time breaking out the pinochle deck. The room we are in is painted all gray and has a bench table to sit around. The lighting consists of four fluorescent lights that made everyone look slightly green. The bunks are 3" thick gray mattress over stretched and tied canvas. When I walked in, the first thing I thought was the floor looked like a better place to sleep. So, this will be our home for the next 5–6 months, but the thought of seeing Europe is so exciting that it seems worth any inconvenience. During the day we can go up on the main deck to get some air. It's quite a sight to see all the helicopters lined up and watch them rising straight into the sky and soar off into the blue. There isn't much else to do but read. Someone gave me "Goldfinger," one of the James Bond books, and that started my quest to read all the Bond books. I felt like we were going to many of the places in the books, and I could see where Bond traveled.

Please don't tell Tim, Jim, and Kim, but I bought them all Marine rings, and I really hope they will like them. I bought both of you something too that I hope you will like. It's time for lunch, so I have to go. The good news is the Navy has great food, so we look forward to chow. I will write again when we arrive in Spain.
Love, George

Dear Mom and Dad,   1/23/64
Last night I returned from shore leave in Barcelona, Spain. Its early morning now, and I am tired but wanted to tell you about the great time I had. In spite of orders to travel in groups, I decided to go this one alone and take in as much as I could, so I went ashore yesterday with just a pint of American scotch and my camera in a backpack. I had no plan in mind when I gave my salute, walked off the ship, and started walking along the waterfront. I must have walked 10 miles taking pictures of the colorful architecture, people, sculpture, and beautiful old fountains.

I realized I was hungry when down a very narrow street I noticed a sign hanging over a bar with the head of a bull. Peering into the window, I saw it was empty except for four guys sitting at a table. I walked in, and they waved me over, so I went to their table and introduced myself. Gesturing at my uniform, someone with a heavy Spanish accent said "American" and offered his hand. They invited me to sit down and offered me ouzo, a Greek liqueur. It tastes like anise and packs a good punch. Remembering the scotch in my backpack, I pulled it out, offered it to the men, and gave a toast. We were feeling no pain when someone said they had been to a bullfight, and a young guy stood up and grabbed a tablecloth and yelled "Muleta!" which I found out meant cape. He started waving it in the air to make gestures like a bullfighter. I put my hands on my head and stuck my two fingers up like bull horns, and they started clapping and yelling. As I charged forward, he swung the cape over my head, and I got caught in the cloth and fell over a bar stool. I was feeling no pain until the next morning when I woke up with some bruises and a bad headache. Someone had found a cab for me,

and with goodnight hugs and back slaps I climbed into the backseat and fell asleep. The driver woke me and pointed me to the ship. Guess your son is a Marine full of bull!
Love, George

Dear Mom and Dad,   2/8/64

Our next port was Naples, Italy, and while on ship I made friends with an Italian American named Frank Russo who we call the "old man" because he looks about 40. Russo is a good-natured guy who laughs all the time even when we tease him. He invited me to tour Naples and meet his uncle who lives there. Naples is an amazing city, famous for art and cuisine and wine, and I loved it. We walked the streets for a while and visited the Zoo di Napoli, which has beautiful tropical gardens and a wide array of exotic animals. We spent the morning watching the animals doing their daily routines and then grabbed a cab to meet Russo's Uncle Angelo, who is a teacher.

    Uncle Angelo took us for a tour of the city through narrow streets and told us some of the history. We visited the Piazza del Plebiscito—the main square where we saw the Royal Palace, the church of San Francesco di Paola, and the Teatro di San Carlo, which is the oldest opera house in Italy. He was an excellent tour guide, and I have pictures to show you when I get home. At the end of the day we stopped at a dockside restaurant for dinner. The waiter dropped off a basket of incredible-smelling fresh bread, and I immediately woofed down several slices. The main course was fish with pasta and fresh vegetables. The seaside restaurants use fish oil instead of olive oil, and it gives everything a very distinctive taste. After dinner we went to Angelo's house, and I met his big noisy wonderful family who immediately offered me refreshments and made me feel at home. I hated to leave, but it was getting late and time to report back to the ship, so Angelo drove us back, and we parted ways with handshakes and hugs. I love Naples and wish you could see it with me. Russo and I boarded the ship, saluted the officer on deck, and headed to our racks.

    Please write and let me know how everyone is doing.
Love, George

Dear Mom and Dad,   3/10/64

This cruise is full of adventures. My friends mentioned that they were taking a bus trip to the Italian Alps to ski, so I went with them. The bus took us from the ship to the Alps. It was a long drive through beautiful country with quaint villages and a view of sharp vertical mountains. We stopped in a small town that looked like a setting for Hansel and Gretel. When we arrived, everyone split up to go shopping or to the local pub, but I really wanted to ski and left them to rent equipment. Because it was a day trip, we were wearing dress greens, and I guess I looked strange on the mountain in uniform on my first-ever attempt to downhill ski! It took some time to master the tow rope, but I finally made it up the mountain and was faced with sheer terror at the prospect of getting to the bottom. About halfway down, interrupted by numerous falls, a young Italian boy noticed I was having a lot of trouble. I guess he took pity on me and offered to give me some lessons. He stayed with me until I got the hang of it, and by the end of the day I had mastered snow plowing. Everyone had stories to tell when we got back to the ship, and I shared my skiing experience, leaving out the comical and embarrassing parts. It was a perfect day. So far this Med cruise has been like a vacation, with liberty in most of the seaport cities and countries. Our next stop will be Athens, Greece.

Will you please send cash if you can because my pay doesn't last long? I'm eating my way through the Med, ha-ha.
Love, George

Dear Mom and Dad,   4/15/64
We just landed in the port of Athens, Greece. Once again, the architecture and fountains are just incredible, though really decayed. Since I don't have much time to tour the city, my first objective was to try the local cuisine. I went to a popular taverna and ordered food that I never had before or knew existed. I started out with a cup of lemon soup and Greek salad called Horiatiki with feta, Kalamata olives, and red onions, and then for my main course I had moussaka, which is layers of meat, tomato sauce, and eggplant with a delicious sauce. It looked something like our lasagna but with a totally different taste. To finish, I had a dessert called a baklava—best thing I have ever tasted! I have decided I love Greek food the best except, of course, your meat and potatoes, Mom. I forgot to mention they gave me ouzo; I love that stuff. I am taking it all in and taking tons of pictures. I really hope I can return someday. Will try to write again before I get back.

Love from your Greek, Italian, and Spanish son,
George

We arrived back in Norfolk, Virginia, on May 24, 1964, after five months on the Mediterranean cruise and were bused back to Camp Lejeune to the routine of cleaning our equipment and the regimen of camp. It was difficult after having so much free time, but I was happy to be stateside and managed to take a few days off to go home and see my parents and friends.

One of our favorite spots at home was a drive-in restaurant called Big Boys in the northeast section of Philadelphia. Drive-in movies and restaurants were the popular hangouts of the day. All the hottest cars would show up and rev their engines as carloads of girls pulled in. We hung out for hours flirting until someone announced a drag race, which would take place on the Boulevard (Roosevelt Boulevard in Philadelphia). Within a few minutes the entire restaurant parking lot would clear out and follow the lead cars to the drag area. The police always knew our location and would show up after a couple of races with sirens screeching and lights flashing, at which point we scattered, except for the lucky ones who had girls. Those cars would find dimly lit streets to park. Wrapped in heated embraces, couples would "make out" until discovered and chased by police who would sneak up on the cars with steamed windows, shine a light into the window, and tap their night sticks on the side of the car with firm instructions to "break it up and get home!"

Sunday dinners were family time when everyone gathered at Mom's dining-room table for more than food. We got caught up on each other's lives and swapped stories, talking for hours until Mom put out the pies and ice cream. Everyone wanted to know about my experience on the Med cruise and generally how I was doing. During all my time away, I think this is what I missed most of all. Those days at home were precious times of no formations, no equipment cleaning, and no one yelling—just freedom to get in the car and go any place, any time. The weeks always flew, and before I knew it, it was time to go back to the regimentation of military life. I drove back to the base so I could have my own transportation.

Dear Mom and Dad,   *6/10/64*
On the way back to the base last week I traveled to the eastern shore of North Carolina. I was sitting on the beach watching the ocean ebb and flow, lost in thought about my summers at Ocean City when an attractive young girl passed by. I watched as she dropped her towel and waded into the shallow surf, the blue water surrounding her lovely form. As the waves gathered force, she lost her balance and got caught up in the undertow. I ran to her and pulled her up and away from the next breaker. Looking up as she brushed off sand, she thanked me and walked back to retrieve her towel. I nodded and turned to leave, when she asked if I was down for the summer. Afraid that I might scare her off by telling her I was a Marine, I just said that I was visiting. I couldn't take my eyes off her beautiful smile. Dropping to the sand next to me, she hugged her legs and stared out at the ocean for several minutes, then she said she was from Virginia and had just graduated from high school. The way she carried herself seemed more mature than her 18 years. We discovered our common interest when she shared her plans to go to art school. I have not really talked to a girl since my breakup with Lynn, and I kept thinking how nice it would be to be able to date her if things were different. But at least I had that one perfect afternoon with her on the beach under the blue sky, watching the surf with no thoughts of anything military. I really wanted to stay longer, but she had to leave, and I was on a tight schedule to get back to the base. Driving home I realized I never got her name, so I think of her as Miss Virginia.
I'm managing to get back into the base routine, but I really miss home and all of you. I also didn't realize how lonely I've been and how much I miss dating and having someone to talk to besides a bunch of barracks buddies. I think we all feel the same way.
Love, George

The chance meeting of a pretty girl provided me with months of reflection on that time, and amazingly I still remember it so well. The local girls do not date the soldiers, so most of the free time is spent on the base having a beer at the enlisted club with other guys, exercising at the gym, watching a movie, or reading anything you can find. Recreational activities off base, meeting girls, and making friends is difficult. Generally, the immediate areas surrounding the base consist of strip bars and pawn shops that cater to young men looking for any kind of fun and often in need of cash. None of that makes for a good combination and can get a lonely soldier into trouble, so I tried to spend my time in other ways, which included lots of exercising to work off my physical urges.

In 1964 and 1965, we voyaged to the Caribbean to practice artillery shooting and logistics for troop landings. We called them Caribbean cruises. Our destination was San Juan, Puerto Rico, which is part of an archipelago made up of four islands. The oldest city in U.S. territory, San Juan is Puerto Rico's capital, biggest city, and economic hub.[1]

Culebra, located twenty miles east of Puerto Rico, was established as a Navy base in the 1930s. Its deep bay was used for various artillery and bombing exercises. It was there I learned how to spot for artillery and call in fire missions. The island was hot and dry, and the smell of explosives was always present. We had no contact with the people of the small town at the opposite end of our camp, but I often think now how much they must have hated the deafening noise and the destruction of their beautiful island. After protesting American military exercises in Culebra, the people finally won their case in 1975,[2] and operations were moved to Vieques, fifteen miles to the southwest. Nearly thirty years later, the U.S. Navy left Vieques as well.[3]

Dear Mom and Dad, 7/1/64
We just landed in Culebra, a small island in the Caribbean, for live training exercises and amphibious landings. The eastern end of the island is the Live Impact Area (LIA), used for targeting live ordnance (bombs and shells). Our job was to coordinate live fire from the forward observation bunker for ships, planes, and artillery. Our company was transported to the island's military base called Camp Garcia by way of a landing ship tank (LST). The ship was built for the Second World War to deliver tanks, men, and equipment directly onto the beach like they did at Normandy. Beaching this ship is an interesting operation. After pulling up as close as possible to the beach and opening the large doors on the bow, a long metal gate is dropped, which becomes a bridge for the men to unload the equipment and disembark. After the landing, the LST has a unique way to depart. Before the ship lands, the sailors drop anchor and let the chain out behind them. When they are ready to leave, the anchor chain is pulled in and the ship is backed off the sand. My guess is they've lost a lot of anchors.

Tucked away in the bowels of the ship is our sleeping quarters. Traveling down and through a series of narrow passageways tests the best of memories, and I just remember thinking that I really wanted to know how to get topside in a hurry if necessary. The LST berthing arrangement gives new meaning to the phrase "packed tighter than sardines" because the guy above you is only about a foot from your face. You can't be claustrophobic on these ships!! The barracks at Camp Garcia are hot, metal Quonset huts. We keep the doors and windows open for what little breeze might blow through.

It's so hot in the huts that we try to stay outside in the shade whenever possible, but it feels like it's over 100 degrees inside, and when we are off duty, we strip down to skivvies and shower shoes. The worst thing is we are surrounded by a beautiful blue ocean, which is restricted due to live ordnance (unexploded artillery) from rounds that landed in the water. At least our cots are more comfortable and a real improvement over the ship, but boy, I can't wait for a night's sleep at home again in my own bed with air-conditioning!

I'll write again soon,
Love, George

Dear Mom and Dad, 8/5/64

We completed our training in Culebra yesterday, and our ship brought us back to San Juan, Puerto Rico, for some liberty. The island has two towns—new San Juan and Old San Juan. I loved Old San Juan with its colorful homes, old forts, and plazas. As I walked down cobblestoned streets through the stepped alleys, I felt a familiar sense of home that reminded me of the back alleys in Philadelphia. The native islanders are the working class, and the people are friendly. Most islanders speak English, so communicating was not difficult. My buddies and I did not have much money, but everything is so inexpensive, and we were able to sample some of the local food and tasted their San Miguel beer.

I walked to the west end of the island to the entrance of the harbor and toured the battlements of Fort San Felipe del Morro, the old fort that still stands on the cliffs of San Juan. I wish you could have been with me to see this wonderful and beautiful place. I have pictures, and I plan on coming back as a civilian.

Love, George

Dear Mom and Dad, 8/14/64

Yesterday one of my new buddies, Tom, and I put together a plan of attack for our last day of shore leave. Tom suggested bringing our civilian clothes in a bag, then going to the Caribe Hilton, changing out of our dress clothes into civvies, and walking into the pool area for some drinks and a look at the girls in swimsuits. He figured no one would suspect we were Marines and not guests. My response was, "Tom, that's not acceptable behavior for two Marines—let's do it!" Tom laughed and said, "Okay, let's get our things together, and don't tell anyone or they will all want to come." We waited until they announced liberty, gave our departing salute to the Navy, grabbed a cab, gave the Marine "Oorah!" then headed directly to the Caribe Hilton by the beach and sat on an old wooden bench while planning our next move.

We noticed a side entrance and shower room next to the pool that the employees were using, so we waited until no one was around, ran into the room, and changed our clothes. Tom watched the outside while I changed, and then I watched for him. So far, our mission was on target. I asked Tom if he was ready, and he gave me a thumbs-up. We waited again for a family to walk into the pool area and hung behind like we were together. That got us into the pool area, and we were almost home free. I *could taste a gin and tonic when from nowhere a huge, larger-than-life attendant came over and asked for our room number (a small detail we forgot). We said that we were guests of (gave a random name) and did not have keys. A big grin crossed his face and, shaking his head, he quietly asked us to leave the hotel. Thinking it wouldn't be prudent to argue, we looked at each other, shrugged, and started to walk out of the pool area. Turning to see if he was still watching, the attendant grinned again and whispered, "Nice try, guys," and gave us a salute. And we thought no one else had come up with the same idea!*

Lamenting our failed plan, we spent the rest of the day walking Old San Juan and finished in a hotel bar. After a few beers, I had to go to the bathroom, so I walked to the men's room and found a urinal. The door opened, and to my shock the barmaid came in and used the other toilet. I realized it was a non-gender toilet and that privacy was not an option, so we just smiled at each other, I finished, and I went back to the bar. Tom laughed and said he told the girl no one was in the room just to give me something to remember. Our San Juan visit was memorable for all the wrong reasons. By the time you get this letter, I will be back in the United States.

Miss you guys, and looking forward to seeing you soon.
Love, George

We arrived back at Norfolk on September 5, 1964, and resumed life at Camp Lejeune. After off-loading our equipment and gear from the ship, we spent the first days at the base checking, cleaning, and storing equipment for our next deployment. So far military life was business as usual.

"GUERRA DE ABRIL" (DOMINICAN CIVIL WAR) 5

My next deployment was to Santo Domingo, the national capital of the Dominican Republic (DR). "Santo Domingo is situated on the Southeast coast of the island of Hispaniola, at the mouth of the Ozama River. The island was founded in 1496 by Bartholomew Columbus, brother of Christopher Columbus. Bartholomew named the island La Nueva Isabela after Isabella I, Queen of Spain. From 1936–1961 it was called Ciudad Trujillo after the dictator, Rafael Trujillo."[1]

Dear Mom and Dad,   5/2/65
I was cleaning and checking our radio equipment in the communication building when an emergency notice came around that one of the M116 howitzer artillery companies was going to Santa Domingo, capitol of the Dominican Republic (DR) to help put down a civil war. Don't be upset, but I volunteered to go to the DR with the artillery company. I will be okay, so please do not worry.

The next day we boarded the troop carrier ship in Norfolk and were on our way to the revolution. Belowdecks the ship is a maze of corridors and rooms, but I finally found my quarters and several familiar faces—guys I knew from the Mediterranean cruises. One of them was Charley, a guy from New Jersey. Charley is a character! He has an immense smile, loves to talk, and always has a joke (usually a dirty one, ha-ha). The days are unquestionably less boring with Charley around. As usual we pulled out the pinochle cards first thing, started a game, and played for most of the trip, but we had separate sleeping quarters and didn't see each other again until we returned from the island.

As we approached the island, I remember thinking, how can a peaceful, perfect place like this have a rebellion? I would give anything to live there, and I was hoping it would be over soon so we could enjoy the island. We were not told much about the revolution and were not prepared for what came next. The infantry is always the first to debark the ship to secure the area. The troop carrier dropped anchor, and the landing craft took the first wave to shore. We had been told that the revolutionaries would not fire on U.S. troops, so that group had no live ammunition and immediately came under fire and suffered casualties. At that point, I was still on board the ship when John, one of the radio operators, yelled to me, "George, we're under fire!" "What the hell??" I muttered under my breath. Word circulated quickly as the gunny gave us the signal to go. Luckily by then the beach was secured, and we started boarding the truck that was waiting to transport us to the CP. Our position was around the Hotel El Embajador on one end of the island that was used by our military and the diplomats who were working on a peaceful resolution. The casualties were taken to the hospital ship, but we didn't get any word of any killed in action (KIA). Needless to say, we are all pretty freaked out, especially knowing it was the luck of the draw that we weren't that first wave out, and I couldn't stop thinking of the men who walked into that trap.

On the second day, three of us were told to drive into town and deliver some packages to another company. Thrilled to get away from the CP for a while, we took off in an old jeep and headed along the coast. The sun was beating down, and we were all dying of thirst by the time we spotted a small hut on the beach. What luck—a beach bar! Jack, our sergeant, said to pull over. I asked what was up, and he said he thought he saw something but not to worry. After making a thorough check of the bar, we ordered three Presidents beers—the local brew—pulled up stools, and sat under the thatched roof facing the white sandy beach and blue water.

I was just thinking this is the life when all hell broke loose! Suddenly we heard a shot, and from nowhere a bullet zinged right between Jack and me. I thought my heart would explode as we ran like hell scrambling to the jeep for cover. You never saw three men move so fast, and not knowing what was going on or wanting to find out, we peeled out of the lot and onto the road in about five seconds, flooring the gas pedal and praying like choirboys! Snipers rarely miss their mark, and it's still hard to believe he didn't hit one of us. We called in the incident to our superiors, leaving out the part about the beer, and got off with a thank-you for reporting. The rest of the drive to deliver the package and back seemed like hours, and we were relieved to be back at the CP with the cannon cockers (that's what they call the guys who load and fire artillery).

Other than the bar incident, we saw no action during our month's stay with the artillery unit and received orders to pull out and return to the States. Later we heard from one of the radio operators that several Marines, many rebels, and some civilians were killed and how lucky we were not to have been assigned to the infantry fighting the rebels. Don't worry, I'm fine, but it looks like I pulled a lucky card. I hope my luck doesn't run out.

I'll write when I get back to the States.
Love, George

Operation Power Pack was the military code name for the U.S. intervention in the Dominican Republic.

In 1963, Juan Bosch was elected president of the Dominican Republic in the country's first free election. Hated by oligarchs and militarists, he was overthrown seven months later, and a year and a half after that the junta that took Bosch's place was overthrown in another coup, which ignited the Dominican Civil War from April to September 1965.[2]

At this stage we were beginning to get the message that this was no longer an exercise. This was what war looks like and what we were trained for. We were prepared, but still in the back of our minds was the persistent reminder that at any time we could be next. I can only imagine the anxiety my parents must have felt as they, along with millions of other Americans—especially those in the military—heard the broadcast and awaited news of loved ones possibly caught in the revolt. Ultimately forty thousand soldiers were deployed to the DR. It became one of the bloodiest conflicts in the DR's history. Forty-four Marines were killed and over 172 wounded. Over one thousand Dominican civilians were killed, and some of our troops stayed until July 1966 to maintain peace and a final withdrawal.

Many articles have been written about this conflict with different views about the United States' involvement. At the time, I was unaware of the politics and magnitude of the revolution, or the danger to the Americans trying to leave the country. Innocent of information being reported all over America, we were simply given orders and required to carry them out.

CURAÇAO   6

The normal daily routine of military life was boring, and I was hoping another cruise would come up soon. Sure enough, as I was reading the bulletin board, I saw an announcement, so I signed up for my second Caribbean cruise. I had enjoyed the last trip to Puerto Rico and really wanted to go back to see more of San Juan and Culebra. What's not to like about the islands—soft white sand, palm trees, tepid shallow seawater, rope hammocks, and a gin and tonic in my hand?

At the end of September, we left from Norfolk, Virginia, for Puerto Rico. What I did not know was that our fleet had orders to spend time in Vieques for some target practice and a little shore leave, then get underway to Curaçao, an island in the Caribbean off Venezuela. Together with Aruba and Bonaire, it forms the ABC Islands, part of the Dutch Caribbean. Located on the southern coast of Curaçao in the Caribbean, Willemstad has two parts, Punda and Otrabanda, separated by Sint Anna Bay. The bay leads into Schottegat harbor, and the Queen Emma Bridge connects the two parts of the city.[1]

> *Dear Mom and Dad,*   *10/8/65*
> *Sorry it's been so long since my last letter. We got orders to deploy to the Caribbean for three months. This ship is basically the same as the one on our last cruise to Puerto Rico and carries about 100 Marines plus crew. Most of the guys were with me on the Med and Caribbean cruises, and it was good to see familiar faces again. There are very few places on board that we can go besides the mess hall and on deck, so we passed the days playing pinochle as usual, and I've gotten pretty good at the game. We made up hand signs and face gestures to let our partner know what cards and suits we had, like hand over your heart for hearts, tapping on the table for clubs, etc. We all cheated and knew it, but anything for entertainment!*

The weather was a mix of sun and rain. We are not allowed on deck, but whenever it stormed, I would grab a life jacket, sneak above, and curl up near a hatch (in case I had to get below in a hurry) with a cup of coffee to watch the waves crashing over the bow and the ceaseless rock and roll of the ocean. For me it's just a peaceful way to pass the time.

It was a short trip from Norfolk to San Juan where we docked for a few days and had liberty. I was anxious for R & R and decided to tour new San Juan this time, taking in the sights all day and sleeping on board the ship at night. In contrast to Old San Juan, which is historic and touristy, it's much like any modern city, with lots of nightclubs and restaurants, including Japanese, which we enjoyed. That only lasted a few days, and we got orders for target practice in Culebra. We just arrived, and I'm unpacking and settling into our Quonset hut. Even though it's October, it is still pretty hot in our hut. My shirt is soaked already, but it's starting to rain, and the tapping on the roof is always a welcome sound, knowing it will soon cool us off a bit. One of our guys just came in with a case of beer—even cooler! Later this week we'll be shooting artillery (M116, 75 mm howitzers) and coordinating naval gunfire at the firing range.

Have to go now.

Love, George

Note: First brought into service in 1920 and designed to be disassembled and transported by horse, the M116 75 mm pack howitzer saw service in World War II, the Dominican Republic, and the Korean and Vietnam Wars.[2]

Dear Mom and Dad,   *11/5/65*

We just finished our training at the firing range and got some liberty. I took a quick shower, put on my khakis—the uniform of the day—and grabbed a cab to town where I discovered the locals having a huge celebration. The entire town was decorated, and people were dancing to island music on a large platform. Among the colorful clothing, I stood out like a sore thumb, but there wasn't much I could do about that, so I just worked my way into the crowd, smiled a lot, and ordered a San Miguel, my new choice of beer. Leaning against the bar, enjoying the taste of the cold liquid sliding down my throat, I watched the men and women dancing together with precision movements I've never seen back home. Braving the stage after a few beers, I managed to get my hips and legs moving in some kind of rhythm that had no resemblance at all to the intricate steps and shimmying shoulders around me. But I was soon doing my own version of an island dance and having a great time.

Feeling no pain after a few beers, I started inching my way into the crowd toward a group of girls when one of the guys pulled me aside and, in broken English, warned me not to get any ideas, so unfortunately any chance of female company was off-limits. I had to leave soon anyway to make it back on time, and though I hated to leave the festivities, I drained my San Miguel, got a cab, and asked the driver to get me back to the ship. As we sped off, I remember looking back at all the colorful lights and hearing the music fade into the distance as I nodded off for the rest of the trip. The driver woke me as we arrived at camp, and seeing two sentries coming my way, I got out of the cab, sucked it in, and walked toward them trying to look sober. Realizing they were friends, I gave a slightly cockeyed salute and accepted their offer to help get me to my bunk. Lucky break!

Miss you.

Love, George

Dear Mom and Dad,   11/16/65

We left Vieques last week and made our way south to Curaçao, arriving midday. It was hot and sunny, and as we approached the southern coast of the island, the aqua water was so inviting I wanted to dive off the ship. I couldn't wait to get a shore leave and check out this beautiful place.

With a quick salute, I left the ship and walked to the center of town, which I learned was Willemstad, Curaçao's historic capital. Everywhere I looked I saw a riot of color, from the pastel-colored colonial architecture to the brightly patterned clothing. Along the waterfront was a tented bazaar area with booths selling food, vegetables, fruits, and local artwork. Even the colors of the fruit and vegetables seemed brighter to me. I walked the streets taking in all that I could, finally stopping for lunch at a little restaurant near the ocean where I had mouthwatering conch soup. As I turned to leave, the harbormaster set off an alarm for the pontoon bridge to open for a cruise ship that passed right in front of me, not more than 20' away. It was completely surreal.

After lunch I found a bench near the waterfront and fell asleep to the sound of the water slapping the wharf. When I woke up, it was late, and I had to get back to our ship before dusk. We were only in Curaçao for a week, and I took advantage of every minute of shore leave and got to know the island well.

Last night was a blast and the best birthday celebration I ever had! We were informed by our commander that the Dutch were throwing a big party and we were all invited. I hoped they knew what they were doing inviting a shipload of jarheads and squids (Navy sailors) to the same party, but I was not missing this for anything in the world! We were bused to a large open area south of town. As we arrived, I could hear steel drums, and it was lit up with colored lanterns. There were several tables piled with local food and plenty of alcohol. I stayed with my favorite gin and tonic, tasted everything in sight, and was soon doing the limbo. Hours went by with no fights—just fun for a change, I think—though most of the details are a blur. I only remember getting on the bus, saluting the ship with the wrong hand, and crashing in my, or somebody's, bunk. This morning most of us in the chow line were hung over and looking for coffee, but I am sure I had a great birthday! We are on our way back to Norfolk today and should be home soon. I will call you when we get back.

Love, George

CALL TO DUTY 7

At the end of my second year of service, I was promoted to the rank of corporal, which is classified as noncommissioned officer (NCO) or "noncom." With my promotion came added responsibilities and a little healthier paycheck. The noncoms are the main link between the commissioned officers and the enlisted. The responsibilities include overseeing the daily routine of the men, including formations and equipment maintenance, and the discipline and morale of the men.

In early 1966, word of the Vietnam conflict filtered down through the ranks and became a continued topic of conversation. Already several friends in our company had been deployed. Returning from the mess hall late one afternoon, I noticed a sign-up sheet for Vietnam on the squad bay bulletin board with a few names penciled in. Already realizing that I could be called up next, I had been giving serious thought to volunteering and headed back to my bunk to decide about signing up for Nam.

Making the decision was not an easy one, but knowing the military would send me sooner or later, I figured volunteering would look better on my military record. Once I signed up, I began to realize what I was facing, and the confidence I had in my decision started to slip away as the reality of war occupied my thoughts. One of the biggest fears of a soldier is how he will react under fire in that split second that could mean killing or being killed or saving a life. I felt sure that faced with that reality, I could rely on my training and sense of self-preservation, and I would readily execute my duty.

With the decision made to volunteer, time seemed to fly, and within a few days I received my orders for Vietnam and started packing. To say my parents were upset and worried when I told them is an understatement, especially my mother, who had been adamantly against my enlistment from the start. In later years, to see her reaction, I kidded that I had volunteered, and it was worse than I had even expected. She had never gotten over the fact that I had enlisted, and I'm very glad she never knew the truth. Maybe some things are better left unsaid.

About the time I volunteered for Nam, the protesting had begun. Thinking back, I realized how little we knew about what we were getting into. The media wasn't yet reporting everything about the conflict except for the action reports, and I was unaware of the antiwar movement. Had I known at the time, I wonder if the controversy would have impacted my decision about enlisting.

I received orders to report to Camp Pendleton, California, for Survival, Evasion, Resistance, and Escape (SERE) training before shipping out to Nam. All Marines destined for Nam had to go through this training. Boy, was I in for a big surprise!

> *Dear Mom and Dad,* *3/25/66*
> *On arriving at Camp Pendleton, I was given a three-day pass, so I rented a car and toured the California coast, spending most of my time walking the beaches. On my last day of leave I decided to make a surprise visit to Grandma who burst into tears when I showed up at her front door. I was amazed that she recognized me right away because I think I was only four or five years old when we were there, but she did and she said how much I look like Dad. She seemed in good health and asked about everyone at home. I was surprised and definitely impressed to hear she still participates in the local women's drill team. She's a feisty little woman!*
>
> *I stayed for several hours, and we just relaxed and talked about my tour and everyone in the family. I really felt bad when I had to leave. She kept hugging me, and it was difficult to say good-bye, especially when it registered that this could be the last time I might see her. Actually, not to be morbid, but if fate is against me during this tour, it could be the last time I see anyone.*
>
> *I made it back to the camp that night, had a beer, and fell asleep. Before I knew it, liberty was over, and they immediately sent us by truck to the nearby mountains for the SERE training. I was told that our military hired British commandos to run the program. We were all roasting from the drive when suddenly the truck stopped and we were ordered to get out. I couldn't help wondering if they somehow managed to pick one of the hottest days of the summer on purpose. With only a bag of rice and a canteen of water, our company was turned loose in the mountains with no instructions except to escape and avoid capture. We definitely were not prepared for this! When I saw the other guys running like hell in panic, I started looking for a place to hide. Dropping to the ground, I tried to shrink into the thick underbrush for cover, held my breath, and attempted to calm my pounding heart. I could hear the commandos getting closer but was completely surprised when, with a thump on my head, I realized they had me.*
>
> *The commandos knew all the possible escape routes, and within 20–30 minutes we were all captured. They corralled us with rifle butts, tied our hands behind our backs, and forced us to march on a deserted road to an unknown location while yelling*

obscenities and prodding us with sticks as we stumbled along eating dust from the guys in front of us.

Located on the top of the mountain, the POW camp was completely open to the scorching sun and surrounded with barbed-wire fencing. We were filthy and dehydrated, and the hours of yelling and punching were taking a toll. Conditions were made worse by periodic gusts of wind. Most of us were choking up dust, and several guys collapsed from heat exhaustion. Our captors packed everyone into a small compound, and with hands still tied behind our backs, they made us kneel in the dirt to wait for individual interrogation. It was all meant to demoralize us and break our spirit, just as the enemy would do to prisoners.

I was at the back of the compound, and as I looked around at the sea of Marines, I realized I could be in that position for hours, so I started inching my way toward the front hoping to be interrogated sooner. I can't remember how long it took, but finally a commando grabbed me and, still on my knees, pushed me in front of the interrogator. As he began firing questions about my company, I remembered our drill instructor's relentless training to only give name, rank, and serial number if captured. I was nauseous and at the point of collapse but managed to resist the verbal assault until, thankfully, it finally ended. But there was more to come.

After the interrogations, we were sent to a holding pen where they separated the enlisted men from the NCOs. We were given water and cigarettes and generally treated better in front of the enlisted men. This was planned to divide the ranks, create dissention, and cause a breakdown in the chain of command. Disobedience, antagonistic behavior, and attempted escape were quickly and swiftly dealt with by harsh punishment. Some of the men who tried to escape but failed were sent to the hotbox. The hotbox is a coffin buried in the ground where men were placed for approximately one hour to simulate what we would experience in Vietnam if caught by the enemy. It was a terrifying experience the commandos tried to make as authentic as possible, and for that we have to thank them. Suddenly the yelling and screaming at boot camp began to make sense too. Immediate compliance saves lives. In battle there is no room for questioning or second-guessing.

As grueling as it was, rest assured that at no time were any of the prisoners in danger. Fortunately, no one was seriously hurt. But the commandos knew what they were doing, and what we didn't know was that they had medics at the camp prepared to take care of any injuries or medical event that might occur. It was mentally and physically exhausting and probably not nearly as bad as an actual capture. We were starting to get the picture of what can happen if you become a prisoner of war (POW), and we realized we have to be prepared for any possibility, including the unimaginable. It is vital to our survival that the training be authentic so the lessons learned will stay with us and may save our lives.

I have to go but will write again when I can.
Love, George

I was able to find several articles documenting the origin of the SERE training. The Air Force developed the training program during the Second

World War. More recently, the program was expanded for Korea and Vietnam. The Air Force realized that soldiers captured and untrained in the tactics of survival were unprepared and in great danger during a high-risk mission. The Air Force implemented the four training modules and coordinated with the Army, Navy, and Marines. SERE is an acronym for:

1. Survival—how to live on the land
2. Evasion—how not to be seen and how to avoid capture
3. Resistance—how to counter mind control (brainwashing) and torture
4. Escape—how to successfully plan a way to freedom

The Marines conducted SERE training at several camp locations, including the Mountain Warfare Training Center in Bridgeport, California.[1]

Recently I was told that the SERE training was eventually shut down for being too hard and realistic. Guys were writing home and complaining about the cruelty of being a POW. As I said in my letter, I was grateful, and I know the training was necessary to prepare us for the realities of what might lie ahead.

Dear Mom and Dad,   *4/2/66*

Just when I thought all the training was done and I could get some much-needed shut-eye, the gunnery sergeant (gunny) came into the barracks yesterday and told us to scramble for another field training exercise. We grabbed our gear and got in the truck headed for—you guessed it—the same mountains we just left from the SERE training. Troops are transported in the back of a 6-by-6 (a truck about 14' long designed to transport a 5-ton load) on long bench seats that hold about 24 guys. No cushioned seating in this baby! He told us this would be a reconnaissance (recon) exercise.

It was getting dark as we finally came to a screeching halt at the top of the mountain. Gathering around the gunny, he laid out our mission—to walk 2–3 miles east of our CP, find the enemy encampment, scout out the weak areas in the perimeter of defense and find the locations of their sentries, and then develop a plan of attack to destroy their forces. He divided us into several teams, and I was put in charge of a six-man team including me.

By the time we moved out, the night was black as tar with a wet blanket of fog obscuring any view. The lack of moonlight actually made good conditions for cover but bad for finding our way back, as we would find out. We walked down the muddy road until we hit the flat land below. Forty-five minutes later we reached a tree line and stopped to regroup. Figuring the enemy camp to be about a half mile on the other side of the trees, we silently proceeded until we came to an open area with a small hill.

Forming the men into teams, I reviewed my plan for the mission. Team One would stay behind and keep a perimeter of defense to capture any enemy forces roaming around the area or act as backup for my team if we ran into trouble. I gave them the password, and the rest of us proceeded south along the tree line about a hundred yards where I had Team Two set up another ambush, then moved Team Three onto the back side of the mountain. Their orders were to send one man out of each team to recon (search) the mountain. After 30 minutes, I would return to each ambush location to collect the teams.

Leaving my position, I began to crawl slowly up the hill though the mud and underbrush. I was breathing hard, and my heart was pounding like a drumbeat as I inched closer. I managed to get close enough to the enemy bunker to hear several men talking. Although I sighted one of the sentries in the underbrush, my visibility was limited, and that was as close as I could get without being spotted and captured. Detecting two additional sentry locations about 50 yards apart, I decided that I had enough info and started crawling back to the tree line.

By then the fog had completely enveloped the ground, providing cover as I made my way back to the regroup area where I gave the password to my team partner. Stooping down I waited for his response, but he didn't answer. Whispering the password again more loudly with no response again, I crept closer. "What the . . . ?!" I hissed, realizing that he had fallen asleep! Instead of having my back, my backup was on HIS back. Waking him with a shove, I gave him a reprimand and listened to his lame apology. Deciding not to report him, I kept thinking that if this was a real-life situation, he could have put all of our lives in danger, and I was too PO'd to talk.

Moving back to the Team Two ambush location, we gave the password and asked them to give their reports. They found two sentry locations and a small building on the north side and estimated maybe five to eight people were sighted near the building. We headed back to the Team One ambush position, gave the password, and got their reports. Overall, we found seven sentries, one building, and approximately eight enemy soldiers. Mission completed, we began to work our way back to the CP with more fog closing in. You could only see about three feet, and I was getting worried. A compass would have been good to have, but we were sent out without equipment and were expected to use our own resources, so I asked the team for a volunteer to scout. We figured how long it originally took to get to the tree line from our CP and used that to gauge the distance. Once again I felt all those years of Boy Scout training outdoors came in handy, Dad.

I gave orders to move out in a horizontal line three feet apart so we could see more terrain and maybe find the dirt road. After 50 minutes—only 5 minutes longer than our trip in—the lead scout stopped, turned around, and said he spotted it. I admit to having doubts, but we made it back to the CP, and I was so relieved I could have kissed that road! By then some of the other teams were already asleep on the ground, so I told the men to turn in for the night while I looked around for the gunny to give my report as instructed. Staring up at me, he groaned but thanked me, said it was a good plan, rolled over, and told me to get some sleep. Easy for him to say! I think I smoked five or six cigarettes just to calm down from the night's activities. So . . . this is a small sample of what lies ahead in Nam. Maybe art school would have been a better choice!

I really miss you guys. Please write.
Love, George

Dear Mom and Dad,   *4/12/66*

After the recon training, we were sent back to camp, and when we arrived, I went directly to the mess hall. I was starving and ate until I almost threw up. That night I went to the NCO club to meet the guys and have a few drinks—well, maybe more than a few. Somehow I made it back to the barracks, where I passed out on my bunk in my uniform with boots and cap on. I slept like a bear and woke up a little late and feeling pretty rough but already dressed for the morning formation. I just needed a splash of water and a few aspirin to come back to life, but I really had to run like hell and barely made it to the parade grounds, which are about a quarter mile from the barracks. With a minute to spare, I did my "dress right dress" and stood at attention, which took all the strength I had. Fortunately the parade was short and we were dismissed, so I dragged myself back to the barracks for a nap.

Later that afternoon, without any warning, we were told to pack and get ready for the truck that would take us to the transport ship for Okinawa. By now we've learned to expect the unexpected and not question anything. I quickly folded all my uniforms and shoved them into my duffel bag, grabbed my backpack, and got on the truck that was waiting in the parking lot. Most of us were still hung over from the night before, and no one said a word. When we arrived at the dock, I was surprised by a sea of white-and-green service caps overtaking the loading dock and soldiers saying good-bye to family and friends. I headed toward the ship and climbed the stairs, and as I turned around and looked back, I thought, "Good God, this is it. We are actually heading out to Nam and leaving the safety of the States." I admit I was getting nervous as hell, wondering what was ahead.

Don't worry about me—I promise to keep my head down! Tell Jean and Joan and my nephews I said bye, and I'll write again soon.
Love, George

I remember thinking a lot about my family and home, and the thought that I might not return was like a heavy dark cloud over me, but I kept it to myself and hoped it would go away. I was twenty-one years old, and I had my whole life ahead of me. Getting wounded or killed was not in my plans. The Marines make men out of boys, and I had grown up a lot in the last three years. Training exercises were over, and the real thing was less than a week away. I had been equipped for war, and I was just hoping I was ready for what was coming.

On April 11, 1966, we boarded a transport ship headed for Vietnam. Actually we arrived in Okinawa, Japan, first, and then in a C-130 cargo plane we flew to Da Nang, Vietnam.

DEAD RATS   8

Transitioning from boy to man is that rare time of life, mixing anticipation and cockiness with uncertainty and fear. Up to this point, I admit to being a bit cavalier and naive about how fragile life can be, but the world was my oyster filled with endless possibilities, and I wanted to get on with it even if "it" had to be war. All I really knew about fighting was my military training of course and what I had seen on TV—not the best representation. No matter how much we drilled and trained, it just wasn't the real thing. But now that we were actually in Nam hearing stories about other guys' combat experiences, it was all I thought about, and I was about to find out for myself.

> *Dear Mom and Dad,*   *4/14/66*
> *I am writing to you from the troop transport ship bound for Okinawa, Japan. After locating my bunk somewhere in the bowels of the ship in extremely tight quarters that, once again, unquestionably fit the expression "packed in like sardines," I discovered that several old pals from Camp Lejeune, the Mediterranean cruise, and Santo Domingo were aboard, and I also met new guys. Jim, who is from California, is a surfer. His descriptions of gliding across the water "catching waves" with the spray in his face and wind blowing his hair remind me of our trips to the beach when we lived in California and make me wish I could experience surfing too. Charley is from New Jersey and spent summers at the shore, so we have a lot in common. He's a real joker, talks constantly, and keeps us entertained with endless stories that help pass the time because there isn't much else going on except for the card games, chow, and sleep.*
> *The truth is I'm nervous as hell about Vietnam, and I know the other guys are feeling the same. We all try not to dwell on what might lie ahead for us, but it's like the elephant in the room we try to ignore. At the end of the day, lying in my bunk, I think about home a lot. I remember our Sunday family dinners and football games with all the guys crammed together in my 8' × 10' bedroom watching the game on my little black-and-white TV. So many things to remember that I took for granted. I just*

want you to know, Mom, how much I appreciated your feeding our crew and putting up with our BS. I guess it's true that we don't know what we've got till it's gone.

Got to go, but I'll write again soon.

Love, George

Dear Mom and Dad, 4/16/66

We finally arrived in Okinawa, debarked from the troopship, and were transported to the air base where they housed us in temporary barracks. I was really hoping to see Okinawa, but there was no time. They issued our combat gear and clothing and immediately sent us to an airstrip where we were herded into a C-130 (cargo plane) that flew directly to Da Nang, Vietnam. We left our dress uniforms and noncombat items in duffle bags to be picked up when we come back from Vietnam—if we come back. But no one wants to admit thinking about that. The flight was very quiet, and everyone had the same expression on their faces—grim.

I will never forget the landing in Vietnam. Our platoon had just arrived in Da Nang as replacements for a company that had been hard hit. As the plane's back door opened, I was taken aback by the rush of heat combined with the overwhelming smell of diesel fuel, jet fuel, and something burning that was gross. We soon found out that it was waste from the latrines, which they burn every few days. Latrine duty is something I will try hard to avoid! Waiting on the tarmac was a transport truck to take us to our camp (M54 5-ton, 6 × 6 cargo and transport trucks are used by all branches of the service). It was riddled with bullet holes, had bald tires, and looked like something from a war movie. Dad, we know what Mom would say—"No way you are getting me into that filthy old truck!" The men didn't look much better—like battle worn and weary. We just stood there staring at them, probably all thinking the same thing, "This is how we are going to look soon."

We traveled south for several hours. I'm not sure what I expected, but I was struck by how overgrown with vegetation the country is. Everywhere we looked we saw rice paddies, and every so often we passed a small village with carts and water buffalo. My immediate impression was that the farmer's life here is very primitive compared to our neighborhood farmers, and it's hard to imagine making a living. I wonder what they would think if they saw our farms and equipment.

Arriving at our camp dusty and dirty, we discovered it was all green. This time green tents, green trucks, green men, and what we would later discover to be green food—ha-ha. We were greeted by our platoon sergeant, a tall guy from Maryland wearing no shirt and a flak jacket with dirty fatigue pants. He had a cigarette dangling from his mouth through his scruffy beard and a stone face that I decided I wouldn't cross. We soon learned you just do whatever he says—quickly! Directing us to our assigned hooch and bunks, he said, "The ones who don't make it home are the new boots and short-timers. Keep your mouths shut, do what we do, and you might just make it back home," as he unceremoniously walked out. It reminded me of the last thing you told me when you dropped me off at the recruiting center when I left for boot camp. He seems to know what he's doing, though, and is actually pretty patient with all of our questions. We found out that his brother is a chopper pilot, and he's hoping to see him in Da Nang soon.

Apparently our company had been hit pretty hard and suffered many casualties during an operation in the Mekong Delta, and I was glad to find out the men we will serve with are mostly seasoned Marines who have been "in country," as they say, for 6–8 months, if not longer. It was completely unnerving to hear that among the hardest hit were radio operators. And it didn't help to learn our command call sign is "Sudden Death." So that means, Mom and Dad, every time I call someone on the radio, my first words are "Sudden Death," a reminder of the grim possibilities.

By the way, the sunsets here are spectacular, like the sky is on fire. It reminded me of evenings at home watching our Bucks County sunsets, just about as beautiful as anyplace in the whole world. A few nights ago, we were on top of a hill sitting around on some old chairs and crates watching the sun go down with a brilliant red-orange glow that stretched as far as you could see. You could easily be fooled into thinking this strange, beautiful land is peaceful. As I stared in awe of the view, I was struck by the deception of the serenity on the mountaintop that belied the grisly carnage just beyond the horizon.

We were told there is a Vietnamese market nearby, and we may get to Da Nang for some R & R, so I could use some cash. Will you please send some when you can? Thanks!

Love, George

Several months after arriving, I received a field promotion to the rank of sergeant to fill a vacancy. Normally it takes three to four years to be promoted unless you are in combat and receive a field promotion. During times of war, rank may be accelerated due to the need for replacements when soldiers rotate out, receive promotions, or are wounded or killed in action.

Dear Mom and Dad,   5/3/66

I have been in country for two weeks now, and so far it's been quiet. The camp is huge, with a sea of tents all over the valley. The mess (cafeteria) is the largest tent. We also have a sick bay, a motor pool, an armory where the weapons are maintained, the officers' tents, and the command post where operations and fire missions are planned. The conditions at the camp are basically hot and hotter, with rain every few days that cools things off slightly. The dirt roads are marked with truck tire ruts that fill with rainwater and create puddles the size of kiddie pools. Then the whole place is a mud pit, and we have to scrape it off our boots with tongue depressors.

Our battalion was regrouping and preparing for an S & D (search and destroy) operation, according to the latest scuttlebutt. Last evening, I was returning from chow when I noticed something in one of the puddles and stopped for a closer look. Someone had dumped 4 or 5 newborn rats and left them to die. There is a real problem with rats getting into our tents and food. They even gnaw on hard surfaces, and they have an odor. So it's a constant battle of soldiers against rats, using any means to kill them—poison bait, man-made traps, and even hitting them with foxtails (a brush that comes with a dustpan).

Even knowing this, looking down at them struggling, they looked so helpless, my first instinct was to save them. But as I watched their efforts to escape the puddle, I recalled an event that happened when I was little that stopped me. I was playing in a vacant lot with some boys when one of them found a nest of robin's eggs and passed it around for us to hold. I remember touching an egg, and it felt slightly warm like there was life inside. I could almost imagine the little beak breaking through the shell and a tiny bird emerging. Before I knew what happened, one of the boys grabbed the nest and threw the eggs against a brick wall. I was horrified, and when I saw the eggs break and run down the wall, I remember feeling like I might throw up. The boys laughed and ran away as I stood at the wall with tears in my eyes thinking, how could that kid just kill something so vulnerable? I wasn't too young to recognize the callous act as an inhuman lack of value for a life, even for a tiny egg holding a bird-to-be. It was not just about hurting a life but also about protecting one, which at the time I couldn't do.

Squatting down watching the rats, I was very tempted to pull them out and save them as I wished I could have saved the eggs so long ago. And this time I had a choice, but something stopped me. The baby birds forming inside the eggs were innocent and a benefit to the world. As innocent as the tiny rats appeared, they would grow up to be invasive and can be quite aggressive and dangerous. More than a nuisance, they terrorize the camp and are our enemy. Somehow in that moment they represented everything I had learned during those months in training about killing to survive. This small, seemingly insignificant act represented the whole war for me and my response to taking lives when needed. The rats represented the Viet Cong that are terrorizing this country, destroying and stealing property, and killing innocent civilians. During war, we kill the enemy so that those threatened can survive, and we must align our minds with that responsibility of taking some lives to save others, while somehow remaining human.

One rat came very close to the edge, and honestly it took some effort not to rescue it. I stood watching as it submerged and a few remaining air bubbles came up to the surface. As the last one died, I thought, "You look harmless enough, but you are our enemy," and I knew I had to keep my perspective with respect to taking a life versus fighting to save lives, including my own. I still worry about how I will react to killing someone if the time comes, especially if face-to-face. But my duty is to fight the enemy and protect the innocent, and I now feel I will be ready.

That's enough for now. Looking forward to hearing from you.
Love, George

The incident with the bird eggs had a lasting effect on me, as did the seemingly casual incident with the baby rats, which I connected as examples of how different circumstances affect our sense of right and wrong as well as our sense of duty. I know it helped prepare me for the enormous task for which I might be called. It was becoming harder to keep my letters home lighthearted. What we were experiencing was taxing our spirits, and details began to tumble onto the pages as my need to unburden and make sense of what I was seeing became more urgent.

> Dear Mom and Dad, 5/10/66
> Recently we went on a search and destroy (S & D) mission north of Da Nang. We had walked several miles in the dry, stifling heat, and I was about the fifth man back. I had my camera with me and was distracted by the scenery. I was taking pictures like a tourist instead of staying on the alert and ready for the mission as my training demanded. Obviously (and stupidly), that we could be ambushed or in a firefight was not my first thought. Being the radio operator and carrying my equipment, I didn't have a rifle, and my pistol was holstered, so if attacked I would be unprepared for an immediate response. Engrossed in the surroundings, I was oblivious to my situation and naively not concentrating on the fact that engaging the enemy could be around the next corner. This lack of connection or concentration for new arrivals (or "boots" as we are called) concerning the possible danger is often why soldiers die when they first arrive. We've been warned that the Viet Cong can be hiding anywhere ready to ambush. Sometimes you need a smack in the face to wake up to reality when the view looks deceivingly peaceful.
>
> Our company stopped on a hillside and sent a squad out to the tree line to search for Victor Charlie (radio ID for Viet Cong)—not to be confused with my friend Charley in a previous letter. While we were waiting for the squad to check in, two H-46 supply helicopters landed in our CP with fresh water, ammunition, and food. When the helicopters landed, the downdraft from the rotors blew dirt into the air, and everything was covered in dust, including us. Not the first time we were eating dust, and I heard someone yell, "If they do that again, I will lock and load!" To our surprise, one of the chopper pilots was our sergeant's brother. They only had a few minutes to see each other, but I know how much those moments meant to the sergeant, and we were happy he had them because here any moment might be our last or change everything forever. Just to show off, the brother did a vertical takeoff maneuver that was quite impressive.
>
> While unloading the supplies, a large white onion dropped to the ground. We hadn't eaten for hours, and I was so hungry, anything looked appetizing. So, because no one else wanted it, I ate the entire thing. Boy, did I pay for it later! All of a sudden I heard gunfire and an M79 (grenade launcher) go off in the area the squad was searching. Just to clarify, Dad, the M79 is a single-shot, shoulder-fired, 40 × 46-meter grenade launcher. The grenade produces over 200–300 fragments with a killing radius of 5 meters (about 16'). Smoke was rising from the burning foliage as the radio started to buzz, "Sudden Death 6 [Sudden Death 6 is our commander], this is Sudden Death 1, over," with chatter about a Charlie ambush and that the squad might need some support.
>
> The squad radioed that they killed three to four Charlies and had no casualties. It's ironic how you can go from calmly taking pictures one moment to casually eating an onion the next and then suddenly to full alert. We learned in training that a soldier can NEVER relax and must ALWAYS be on full alert, and now we are living that reality. Believe me, I got the message! The rest of the mission was uneventful, and,

needless to say, that will be the last time I ever have my camera while on an S & D mission.

Time for chow (no onions!). I'll write again soon.
Love, George

Dear Mom and Dad, 5/14/66
A few days ago, our platoon was sent to Da Nang to guard a high-ordnance depot loaded with 6,000 tons of ammunition and explosives, which is crated and stored on pallets and racks in a two-story building. Can you imagine guarding an ammunition dump in a war? Charlie's mission is to blow it up, which makes us a prime target. We had four-hour rotating shifts walking the building's exterior to make sure it was secure, and we couldn't wait to get back to our hooch. May in Nam is normally about 100 degrees, and all we think about is stripping down to our skivvies and shower shoes to keep cool. Not a pretty sight!

Across from the dump was a small village that was set up as our CP with a make-shift mess hall and areas to bivouac (rest). The lieutenant told me to go and get some chow and then come back to relieve him so he could eat. I wasn't really hungry, which is rare for me, but I walked over to the mess tent for some Kool-Aid and then headed back to relieve the lieutenant. About 20 yards away, out of nowhere, a fighter airplane came in from the sun over the river and strafed our position (that is the term for rapid fire from an airplane), then fired a rocket into the mess tent that I had just left. I was standing in the middle of the courtyard with no protection and started to run like hell as the lieutenant, who had taken cover in one of the houses, yelled at me to take cover also. As I turned and looked back, to my horror I saw the mess tent in flames and a dark cloud of smoke billowing overhead. For a moment it was like one of those eerie, slow-motion scenes in a movie, then abruptly the camp was chaos, with Marines running everywhere. On the ground, several wounded men were screaming for help, and out of the corner of my eye I saw the ghastly images of open wounds and bloody uniforms. If I had stayed to eat and not left the mess tent, I would have been one of them. Once again, calm, ordinary events of the day became crisis and bedlam, and seconds became hours as I ran for cover near the lieutenant and grabbed my M14 rifle. When the second plane came in, we fired as the pilot strafed us. Then all of a sudden, he broke off the attack. Someone must have radioed the pilots that we were Americans, and they left before we could shoot them down.

Several men and medics rushed to the mess hall and pulled the wounded out from under the tent. One Marine was put on a stretcher, and as they raced by me to the medevac helicopter, I could see hastily wrapped bandages dripping blood onto the ground. I can't lose the images in my mind of bones protruding under the knee where his leg had been severed. They must have given him several shots of morphine, so thankfully he was out of it. Seconds later, the medics rushed another Marine to the waiting helicopter. His head injuries were so severe that part of his head was torn open and bleeding profusely. I couldn't imagine how anything could be done in the field hospital to save the life of this young man. The medics who heroically treat men with *agonizing, life-threatening injuries every day under dangerous and perilous circumstances are the true heroes of this war.*

Altogether we had eight casualties from the attack. I'm not sure how many survived. I was horrified and raging with anger against the pilots, and seeing those Marines wounded and not being able to help them made me feel completely helpless. The reality of this war is sinking in hard and fast, and it's terrifying even if we don't say it out loud.

We stayed for another day, and then we received orders to rejoin our battalion. The following days back at our camp were very somber, and no one talked about what happened. We went on with our business, cleaning our weapons and radios and writing letters home because that was all we could do. But I still keep seeing that explosion. I can hear the roar of the plane as it flew in and see it shoot rockets on the mess hall. I can hear the explosion and the screams as men were hit with shrapnel. I still see the blood and the men lying on the ground crying out for help. But more than that, I keep wondering about their fate. Did the man with the head injury survive, and how will his family cope with the news? How will the man who lost his leg recover from such a trauma, accept his fate, and go on with his life? How will it affect his family and maybe girlfriend or wife? In their place, I'm not sure how I would handle it, or even if I would want to survive. I need to get those faces and these thoughts out of my head so I can keep doing my job. This was near miss #2.

Miss you and the family very much.
Say a prayer for me.
Love, George

One minute we are doing ordinary things, and the next minute the war is in our lap. We mentally switch gears for our sanity and survival. This is what they prepare us for. The training in boot camp—endless hours of marching, mission preparation, hand-to-hand combat, survival training, unquestioned discipline, and the ultimate transformation into a fighting machine—prepares us for a split-second response. At the time, there was no help for how to deal with the trauma of those experiences. Some men reach out to the chaplain, but most men keep it locked away for years, some permanently, and rarely is it discussed with family. As I now unlock these compartments, I see pictures of that time and place as vividly now as they were then. Setting down these words, while reopening long-closed wounds, begins to release repressed feelings of terror and anger.

What we didn't know at the time was that the Buddhists with the South Vietnamese military, on the one hand, and the South Vietnamese government (primarily Catholics) on the other, were having a civil war. "It started when General Thi (Buddhist) was removed by the South Vietnamese government (Premier Ky) in March 1966, and then large crowds of Buddhist protestors rallied in the streets of Da Nang. The Buddhist protestors called themselves the 'Struggle Movement.' The Movement had a resentment of the South Vietnamese government and the United States as well. By late May the Buddhist force had taken and held several key locations in Da Nang."[1]

After some extensive research, I found out that two South Vietnam Air Force (VNAF) fighter planes had targeted the Buddhist Struggle Movement troops that were in a compound near the armory and our village. The VNAF claimed that the rockets that blew up our mess hall had fallen short of an Army of the Republic of South Vietnam (ARVN) position near us, and the strafing was not mentioned. Fallen short, my ass. Did I mention we were guarding an armory with live ammunition inside? The fighter plane that attacked us was a prop-driven Douglas Skyraider A-1, an old-style fighter that the VNAF was using out of Da Nang, often called the "water buffalo" during the war. The action report indicates that eight Marines were wounded in the attack.

It is hard to believe that we had two wars going on at the same time—the Viet Cong (VC) and the Buddhist/Catholic civil war. "Every day the civil war threatened to draw the United States closer to another intervention that would cost more lives and confusion. On May 27, 1966, Premier Ky and General Thi arranged a meeting to call an end to the civil war, with General Thi stepping down. It still took more time for the Buddhists and Catholics to calm down. But never to be forgotten is the horrific tragedy when several Buddhists poured gasoline on themselves and set themselves on fire in protest of General Thi stepping down."[2]

We were like the blind men and the elephant whose perception of truth was limited to their experiences. Knowing only what we were told or happened to hear, our version of the truth of the conflict was far removed from reality.

CHUCKLES 9

In my letters, I often refer to sitting around cleaning our equipment. Although this was one of the few activities we had to do and it became sort of a ritual, it was also crucial to our very survival. Weather conditions in the field affect equipment immediately. Dust, mud, rain, and water from wading through streams can cause equipment to fail. Carbon buildup reduces performance, and weapons jamming is a big fear. It is necessary that all equipment be maintained in top-notch working condition.

Several weeks had passed since the action at the Da Nang armory, and we were all on edge. Not that we were looking for action but just something to break up the monotony.

Dear Mom and Dad, 5/26/66
Today around 5:00 p.m., right after we finished some chow, a few of us decided to clean our weapons. We were sitting on some discarded wooden fruit crates talking about home. The guy next to me was a boot, newly assigned to our company. You can tell a boot just by his greens, still pressed and clean, unlike the rest of us in "seasoned" attire. He was a loudmouth and a bit of a know-it-all—the type who acts like he could win the war by himself. He was loading his Colt .45, and I noticed he was careless where he was pointing the gun. Before I could say anything, bang!! the gun goes off. You guessed it—he shot himself in the leg. Not knowing what had happened, the entire camp went into immediate defense mode. Within seconds, 20 men were running for cover or jumping into foxholes, and those in or near their hooch were grabbing for their weapons. As someone shouted an "all clear," one of the guys pulled off his belt and tied a tourniquet around the boot's leg while we yelled for the medic. The boot was screaming and dripping blood. The medics came with the stretcher and carried him off after checking and dressing the wound. I felt bad for the guy and hoped he would be okay, but, truthfully, we were all pretty pissed off, thinking we were lucky that the fool didn't shoot one of us! I guess that was near miss #3. Bad enough we have to worry about VC and sappers without being killed by our own. Seems like we are either sitting

around bored to death, dodging death, or facing down death in the field. Letters from the normalcy of home are the only relief from this insanity.

Please keep writing.
Love, George

A few days later, we were told that the boot was under investigation for possibly shooting himself intentionally to get out of Nam. We heard stories about guys shooting themselves to get out of combat but never saw anyone do it until now. I still think it was a careless accident but never really found out what happened and never saw him again. Most likely he was assigned permanent burn-pit duty (large in-ground fire pits to dispose of human waste and camp trash).

Dear Mom and Dad, 6/10/66
We received orders on May 30th to move north of Da Nang where we made camp in an area called Phu Bai. It's about an hour from Da Nang on top of a large hill. It overlooks most of that area and gives us good protection from Charlie.

Last week our company went out on an S & D mission. We walked for most of the morning and entered a deserted hamlet, known to be under VC control, that had been hit with napalm bombs. Most of the huts were burned-out shells. On the side of the road, we passed a dead VC—my first look at the enemy. The body was black and decaying; the clothes and flesh were seared to a grotesque, statue-like figure. It was almost impossible to believe this charred corpse had been a human being. As I looked back at the grisly sight one more time, it surprised me that I felt nothing for this horrific display of lost life. I felt detached, as though watching a war movie, and it was a scary feeling.

We left the area and went on with our mission, walking several miles to a field where we set up our CP. It was an uneventful mission and no live VC were encountered, so we returned to our camp and routine activities. No one spoke of the dead VC that night. We were all bone weary, and most of us turned in early, hoping for a dreamless sleep which was a long time coming. Sometime during the night, I had a dream that I was the villager running from a napalm strike that took out the entire village. It was so real I could feel the intense heat and woke up in a sweat. Unable to shake off the unsettling feeling, I grabbed my pistol and sat staring off into the darkness of the tent for what seemed like hours until, overcome with exhaustion, I finally curled up and slept until reveille.

By then I had discovered three guys I knew from Camp Lejeune who were also radio operators. The next night my friends and I puddle-jumped to the mess hall for dinner where, to my happy surprise, they were serving steak and potatoes—at least that was what the sign said. The steak turned out to be rolled-up Spam, and the potatoes were sticky globs that might be good to fill the cracks in our hooch to prevent the rain from leaking in. Someone definitely had a sense of humor. "Huh!" I scoffed. "They must think Marines will eat anything put in front of them." They were right. We were starved and soon scarfed it down.

With our dining experience ended, we headed back to our hooch. There is a hill just behind with a great view of the countryside where we joined the sergeant and a group of Marines who were lounging on chairs, ammo crates, and busted aviator seats, sharing a case of American beer. It was still hot, and all of us had stripped down to skivvies, boots, and helmets and the beer was going down easy. Before leaving the hooch, I grabbed a pack of Chuckles from C-rats I had. The pack consisted of five flavors of jelly candies coated with sugar. Black licorice and cherry are still my favorites. Of all the treats in the C-rat food box, Chuckles were the most prized and were actually worth money on the black market. Setting the package down beside me, I was saving it to enjoy after I finished my beer. As the sun set, displaying its breathtaking brilliance, we were all lost in thought, knowing that somewhere on the other side of that sun our families and loved ones were probably thinking of us also, wondering and worrying about our days and praying for our safety.

Suddenly, with shocking intrusion to our reverie, someone yelled INCOMING!! Without a thought, I made a beeline for the nearest foxhole and dove in, almost landing on the sergeant. We immediately made ready our weapons in case of a sapper attack. "Oh crap!" I yelled, remembering that I had left my Chuckles on my chair. Without thinking, I scrambled out of the foxhole, with the sergeant shouting, "Where the hell are you going?!" Racing the short distance back to the hill, I grabbed the Chuckles and ran back to the hole. As I dove back in, two VC mortar rounds went off in our CP. Fortunately no one was hurt, but the water buffalo took a direct hit and blew up, spewing water everywhere. So much for showers! I was afraid to look at the sergeant, who was fuming. As we climbed out, he held out his hand. I knew not to utter a word as he took my Chuckles and gave them out to the other guys. Close call #4 and another lesson learned! Whenever I see a pack of Chuckles, it triggers memories of that stupid move on the hill six weeks into our time in Vietnam. Afterward, I remembered what the sergeant had said about how new boots and short-timers are the first to go. In a few weeks our battalion will move north to Phu Bai and then on to Dong Ha.
Love, George

I did a little research and found that the older C-rations were replaced by the Meal, Combat, Individual (MCI) rations, but we still called them C-rats. I remember there was a crazy assortment of meals, like ham and eggs, ham and lima beans, spaghetti, and canned ham, each including a dessert if you were lucky, like pound cake or fruit cup. Not really the food of champions. I think the salt content in the dinners was over 2,000–3,000 mg. I guess that's why they last so long. My favorite was the spaghetti, and believe me, it's an acquired taste. We saw a lot of C-rats in the black market being sold by street merchants to the locals.

Dear Mom and Dad,   6/12/66
We seem to be doing S & D every couple of days now. On Monday we were walking along a ridge when the demolition experts decided to blow a 500 lb. unexploded bomb. One problem—they forgot to warn us. When the bomb went off, it shook the ground

like a level 10 earthquake, and the sound of the explosion was deafening! I felt and heard a zinging sound as a piece of shrapnel whizzed by my left leg. That scared the you-know-what out of me. I was lucky the shrapnel missed me, or I might have lost my leg. No one was hurt, but that was a very close call. I am having a little trouble hearing after that, but my luck continues to hold out so far. That was near miss #5.

We continued on with our mission to flush out suspected VC and set up our CP on a hilltop overlooking farms and villages. Our mortars were being used for a fire mission. One of the mortar guys yelled out, "Hang fire!" (a mortar that did not shoot and is lodged in the mortar barrel). They did something to get the round to shoot, but unfortunately the mortar was aimed straight up, and that means it's coming back down—to us! We all took cover except one of the grunts. He only had time to pull his poncho over his body and pray. The round came back down and exploded in our CP. Somehow no one got hurt, but we thought for sure the guy was dead. Expecting the worst, we approached and were totally shocked to see him stand up. Quivering in his poncho, which now had a dozen shrapnel holes, he unbelievably had only a few scratches. Miracles happen!

Must "di-di" now (Vietnamese for "have to go").

Love, George

Dear Mom and Dad, 6/17/66

Today I ran into a fellow radio operator who told me an incredible story that was going around about a recon team that was sent to Hill 488, west of Chu Lai. The team was dropped by helicopter on the top of Hill 488 to report North Vietnamese Army (NVA) movement in the valley below. The platoon was spotted and attacked by NVA battalions who were trying to take the platoon's position. With most of the men wounded and low on ammo, they continued fighting and were throwing rocks, firing captured weapons, and fighting hand-to-hand combat to prevent the enemy from overrunning their position. Somehow they managed to hold the hill until relieved the morning of the 16th. I could only imagine the terror those Marines must have felt, something they will never forget. I wonder if we'll ever get used to it.

You can't imagine how much we appreciate hearing what's happening at home. When we have nothing else to do, that is all we talk about. I realize how much I'm missing—everyone at home, seeing the boys, hanging out listening to rock and roll with Joan. A couple of guys have radios, but other than crickets chirping, there is not much music here. Sounds like Jean is doing well with her art. I look forward to seeing her work. Please give my love to all.

Love, George

P.S. I got the tape recorder you sent me. Thanks! Great idea! I feel like it restores my soul to hear voices from home in the middle of this madness.

At the time, I only knew what the radio operator could tell me about Hill 488, but I never forgot the story and promised myself that someday I would find out what really happened. I found two articles, one at the National

Museum of the Marine Corps on one of the glass Vietnam panels and one on the Home of Heroes internet site used here with their permission. It is an incredible story of survival and heroism. Please take time to read it in honor of those Marines.

Chu Lai, Republic of Vietnam, 13 June 1966

It was the early days of the United States' involvement in the war in Vietnam. There had been battles and already 21 Americans had earned Medals of Honor. But nothing could have prepared the veteran Platoon Sergeant in Company C, 1st Reconnaissance Battalion, 1st Marine Division, for the nights to come. Everyone knew the enemy controlled the areas west of the base camp at Chu Lai, and recent intelligence reports indicated large troop movements and buildups beyond the relative safety of the Marine outpost. It was time to strike back and prove to the enemy that they were on "Marine Corps Turf."

The sun was falling behind the western horizon as the helicopters moved quickly to the top of Hill 488, then flew back to the base camp leaving behind Staff Sergeant Jimmie Howard, his fifteen Marines and two Navy Corpsmen that completed the small unit delegated to the mission of watching for enemy troop movements in the valley below and calling in artillery and air strikes on them.

For two days Howard and his men did their jobs well. The North Vietnamese control of the area was disrupted by the effectiveness of the American firepower. It didn't take the enemy long to figure out that there had to be someone in the area watching them, directing fire upon their every move. By the third day Howard's Battalion Commander A. J. Sullivan began to sense the danger the small recon patrol faced and offered to pull them out. S/Sgt Howard believed he could hold out one more day and requested permission to remain on the hill. By the time word reached Chu Lai that a full NVA battalion of 200–250 well-trained soldiers were moving on Hill 488, it was too late to pull Howard and his men out. Somehow, they would have to survive the night.

Outnumbered

It was June 15, 1966, and everyone in the patrol knew it was coming. S/Sgt Howard placed all of his Marines in strategic positions around the summit of the almost barren hilltop, with orders to pull back into a tight perimeter the moment the enemy struck. That moment came at 10 o'clock at night, only 12 feet from one of the Marine defenders. As the enemy swarmed the hill amid gunfire, grenades, mortar and support from four .50-caliber machine guns, Howard's men pulled back into a tight circle only 20 yards in diameter.

Back-to-back they began to defend their small perimeter, counting on each other to work as a team to do the impossible. S/Sgt Howard moved among his men, encouraging them, directing their fire, shoring up the weaknesses in the perimeter. For most of his Marines it was the first major test of combat. Huddled in the darkness amid the crash of grenades and mortars, the sky filled with tracer rounds, and outnumbered more than 10 to 1; the leadership and inspiration of S/Sgt Howard was all that sustained them.

Then quiet engulfed the hill as the enemy pulled back, their fanatical human wave assault initially repulsed. S/Sgt Howard looked around him. Every one of his young Marines and both Corpsmen had been wounded in the initial attack. Several were dead. Worse, he knew that the enemy would return in force again at any moment. Grabbing the radio Howard told Colonel Sullivan back at Chu Lai, "You have to get us out of here." But no rescue force could reach Howard's men that night . . . the Marines would have to hold out until dawn.

Then, from down the hill the enemy began to taunt the few survivors on Hill 488 shouting into the darkness, "Marines, you die in an hour."

One of Howard's Marines asked, "Can we yell back at them?"

With nothing to lose Howard told his brave young men, "Sure, yell anything you like." They did, and soon their taunts back to the enemy were met with gunfire. The enemy was preparing to swarm the hill once again. Then the beleaguered Marines caught the enemy off guard as they joined voices in a "horse laugh." Later S/Sgt Howard said, *"They were shooting at us and when we started laughing they stopped. There was complete silence. I think it had a chilling effect on them. They must have known we were terribly outnumbered, but here we were laughing at them"* [italics added].

S/Sgt Howard knew the quiet wouldn't last long, however. He surveyed what remained of his Marines and found that ammunition was running low. The grenades were gone, expended to push back the first wave of the assault. So Marine Corps Staff Sergeant Jimmie Howard issued one of the most unusual combat orders in recent history . . .

"Throw Rocks!"

As incredible as the order sounded, it worked. When the enemy soldiers began to push their way through the sparse brush and knee-high grass to probe the perimeter, Howard's men threw rocks at them. Mistaking the rocks for grenades, the enemy soldiers would move quickly into the open, allowing the defenders clear shots that made every round of remaining ammunition count. For five hours the enemy alternated between small probes and full-scale assault on the surviving Marines. S/Sgt Howard continued to encourage his battered platoon, direct their fire, and calling in aerial support. At times the fighting was hand-to-hand, the enemy so close that Howard directed aerial strafing runs within 30 feet of his position.

From Chu Lai Colonel Sullivan listened to Howard's calm, precise voice across the radio. Then, shortly after 3 A.M., the radio went dead. At Chu Lai there was dread . . . the assumption was that Howard was dead . . . his brave platoon wiped out. Shot in the back, S/Sgt Howard wasn't dead, but he couldn't move his legs. As the enemy continued to assault his perimeter the wounded leader did his best to encourage his Marines. He kept reminding them that if they could just hold out until daylight, more Marines would come and pull them out of there.

Rescue Mission

As daylight dawned a helicopter approached the hill. The Marines were still taking fire, the battle wasn't yet over. The chopper was shot down and the pilot killed. At dawn a Marine company began the trek to relieve the remnants of Howard's platoon. Two more Marines were killed, and it wasn't until noon that they finally reached Howard's perimeter on Hill 488. Five of the defenders on Hill 488 were dead. A sixth died en route to the base camp at Chu Lai. When finally the rescue effort reached S/Sgt Howard and his men, among the 12 survivors there remained only eight rounds of ammunition.[1]

Dear Mom and Dad, 6/18/66
We were on another S & D, and I was assigned to a rifle squad to check out a small village for reported VC activity. We moved out from our CP and traveled a few miles down a dirty, dusty road in oppressive heat, and I was sweating through my fatigues! Twelve of us were walking in two ranks, one on each side of the road, with our weapons at the ready. I was behind the two lead riflemen when a shot rang out, and then one of the Marines on the other side of the road fell to the ground. The others called over to us that one of the riflemen had been shot in the head by a sniper, and I immediately called the medevac helicopter. Meanwhile our medic tried to save him. But he was killed instantly and never knew what hit him.

The sniper was hiding in the tree line and had us pinned down. The area we were in was wide open, with only a couple of low bushes and a few trees. Everyone ran and dove for cover anyplace they could find. Lying in a gully with my radio on my back, I managed to call for support. Waiting seemed like forever while we tried to conceal ourselves to avoid being seen. A second call came in, and as I sat up to answer the call, a bullet zinged by my head. I felt the air move by my left ear, and in a split second I became one with the ground! This is the second time I dodged a bullet, and it's hard to believe that two snipers have missed me so far. This was the closest one yet and my 6th near miss! But who is counting?

The rest of our company joined us, and we set a perimeter of defense. I heard the medevac chopper call in on the radio for smoke (a canister or bottle of colored smoke we throw out so they can identify the landing zone), so I ran out to a clearing and threw the smoke bottle out, then radioed the pilot that it was a hot landing site and to be careful. As the chopper landed, the VC fired on it. The other squads caught up with us and heroically charged the VC sniper positions near the village, killed the sniper, and secured the area. Add one more to the enemy's body count! Fortunately, we only had a few casualties, but unfortunately one Marine was killed, and another family will be getting the dreaded letter. Our "day's work" was done, and we marched back to our camp. Sometimes it's hard to believe this is all real, and I keep expecting to wake up from the most terrifying dream I've ever had.

Back in my hooch in one piece.

Love, George

Dear Mom and Dad, 6/22/66

Yesterday we were on a patrol with the Vietnamese army (ARVIN) to search for suspected VC, but after an entire day we found none. Our commanding officer (CO) told us to check out a local village about a mile down the dirt road while the ARVIN took up the perimeter security. The village was vacant, so after checking for booby traps (which the VC often leave in empty hamlets), we set up our CP. It was hot, and we were tired from walking all day, so I was happy to find a hut that had a hammock in the back. After cleaning it and setting up housekeeping, I gratefully fell into the hammock hoping for some shut-eye. Lying there it occurred to me that I was occupying someone's home, as humble as it was, and I began to feel uneasy about taking it over so casually.

Where was the family, and why was this entire village gone? I was trying not to think about women and children with no home, or worse. Out of respect, and also thinking how dangerous this could be if there were any undiscovered booby traps, I left the house and slept on the ground near the ARVIN forces. I slept with one eye open and my .45 at the ready. Nothing happened during the night, so I was able to get a little sleep. In the morning we moved out and walked back to our camp.

Outside our camp, the local villagers set up a makeshift market with trinkets, food, and clothing. I noticed some C-rats for sale, and remembering they are sold on the black market, I couldn't help wondering who the hell would pay for that. We have to eat them, but for them it is better than starving.

Since I have been in Nam, I could not help but notice that the women were chewing something, and when they smiled their teeth were all black. I'm not sure what it was, but it wasn't a very pretty sight. They seemed friendly enough, but I am sure some of them are VC who would try and kill us if given the opportunity. I decided to skip shopping and returned to my hooch, found a book, and tried to relax.

I hope all of you are okay. Please send more tapes when you can and say hi to everyone for me. Sitting around in this heat reminds me of back home with the boys swimming in the pool, roughhousing, and eating hamburgers on hot summer days. Thinking about them from here makes me realize how much they mean to me, and the summer memories feel very distant. I'm trying to think of something to bring home for them—maybe C-rats, ha-ha!
Love, George

While in Vietnam I noticed that most of the local people, especially the farmers, seemed to have black gums. At the time I wasn't sure why, but it's not very appealing. I later found out it was called betel nut, which after years of chewing turns the gums reddish black. Apparently it's a mild narcotic and can be addictive, but it helped relieve gum and tooth pain in the absence of proper medical and dental care.[2]

Though we had plenty of alcohol and cigarettes, I never tried any drugs. I had a limited knowledge of drug abuse, but there was talk of soldiers using marijuana and worse. Apparently there were growing problems with drugs at home that I would learn about when I returned.

SUDDEN DEATH   10

Every so often, replacements arrived at camp. The new ones looked like poster Marines. We were always glad to see a new radio operator, as our team kept getting smaller and smaller after every operation. Some were being rotated home, and some got wounded or killed.

Dear Mom and Dad,   *7/5/66*
I recently made friends with a new arrival named Paul Reed. He is a corporal and radio operator like me, but he is also a field fire direction coordinator. That means he directs field artillery, air strikes, and naval gunfire. We started talking over beers (I probably already told you we have beer rations that they distribute in camp) about the usual stuff—girls, home, our future. Everyone is always talking about their futures and hoping that they have one. I want to go to a commercial art school, but Paul is thinking of staying in and becoming an officer. He has a younger sister and a brother who also happens to be in Nam, which is very unusual. He has a girlfriend, but they agreed to discontinue the relationship until he returns from Nam. Paul is from Roanoke, Virginia, which is about a 6–7 hour drive from Pennsylvania, and our plan is to meet up after the war, maybe in DC.

Our battalion was just sent north to a place called Dong Ha, where we made camp in an old airstrip and some bombed-out buildings. Not much to say about Dong Ha except the word "dung" kind of describes the camp. We can hear the artillery rounds going off in the distance, which means the North Vietnamese Army (NVA) is not too far. It probably sounds crazy, but we hear so much artillery fire that it's sort of like background noise, and we're (almost) immune to it. We try to go about our business knowing, but not wanting to think about, the fact that people, including our men, are getting killed out there while life goes on normally here. Guys leave every day and come back in one piece, or wounded, or not. It's what we do, just like going to work and at the end of the day returning home, leaving work behind. But our reality returns when the top sergeant appears and yells, "Gear up—we're moving out!" and we immediately get ready to leave for what have become weekly S & D missions.

It's hard to believe that I have been in Nam for over three months now and I'm still in one piece. Yesterday I was sitting on my bunk reading one of your letters when one of the guys yelled that an F-4 Phantom jet had radioed in that he was "bingo fuel." He was running out of fuel and heading for our airstrip to a "dead-stick landing," which means his engine was gone and he was gliding in. Knowing our airstrip was too short for an F-4 landing, I ran outside to see the Phantom coming in fast and low. Thankfully, he landed on the runway. He was trying to slow down but, unable to stop, he flew right past me and went off the end. The jet plowed nose first into a dirt field, creating an enormous cloud of dust. Without thinking, I started to run toward the plane to help the pilot but forgot about the VC wire (barbed wire surrounding our camp used as perimeter defense to keep out the VC). I hit the wire full speed, and my legs got tangled in the fence. I was bleeding badly when I noticed that the other guys had gotten to the pilot and pulled him free.

It feels like there is carnage all around us. It happens out of the blue with guys getting shot, blown up, and killed in seconds. At any moment life can change drastically or end. This time the pilot caught a lucky break. We all did. That plane was about 50' from where I was standing and could have missed the runway and crashed into the camp or blown up. I went back to my tent and pulled out my field first-aid kit. Fortunately, the wire had not cut too deep, and I was able to stop all the leaks with a few bandages. Don't worry, I am okay, just embarrassed—again. I guess this was near miss #7.
Love, George

Dong Ha is the capitol city in the Quang Tri Province, north of Da Nang and close to the Demilitarized Zone (DMZ). The location gave it strategic importance for supporting Marines along the DMZ and monitoring NVA movement. The NVA and Marines were increasing their forces near the DMZ. We knew that the NVA had already crossed the DMZ and infiltrated South Vietnam with the objective of taking Quang Tri as an NVA foothold in South Vietnam.

Due to the airstrip, our camp in Dong Ha was extremely valuable for receiving supplies and troop support. Noticing the large quantity of incoming supplies and troops, we knew something big was being planned and that we would be a part of it. I remember how quiet it got as the men sensed the pending operation.

Dear Mom and Dad, 7/20/66
*I'm writing to you from a mash unit **(I am ok)**. Last week our battalion went on an operation called Hastings. You may have read about it in the papers or seen it on the news. Three days before the operation I got violently ill with the Asian flu and was completely dehydrated. I couldn't sit up without feeling nauseous. The gunny said they would get a replacement radio operator for me, but I insisted that I would be okay for the next operation. The gunny said if I could not complete the mission and someone else had to carry my radio, he would bust me down to corporal. I really thought I was okay, but apparently I was a ticking time bomb.*

A few days later our gunny said we didn't have air transport to get us to the next operation and back, so as usual we had to walk toward the DMZ. We found ourselves fighting our way through a dense, wooded area thick with underbrush in heat well over 110 degrees that was unbearable. Being dehydrated from the flu, I drank my three canteens of water quickly, and my uniform had more water in it than I had in me. To make matters worse, the VC had torched the underbrush behind us. A small breeze was carrying the billowing cloud in our direction, and we were practically crawling to push forward to avoid the toxic smoke. But somehow we managed to get to an open area.

I was in bad shape when I saw a small pond of water. Like an oasis in the desert, I ran for it, completely forgetting the warnings about the possibilities of contaminated water. Before I could drop to the ground to drink, I was stopped by a grunt who pulled me away. That almost put me over the edge until I learned that the water had been poisoned. Fortunately, he had already tested it, so I was damned lucky! We were at the base of a hill, and the CP was being set up on the top of the hill only a few hundred yards away from me. By then I was desperate for a drink and starting to hallucinate about having an ice-cold beer. I could see the beads of cold water running down the side of the can, almost taste the refreshing liquid, and feel it slide down my throat. I managed to get within 20 feet of the top of the hill when I collapsed and passed out. I only remember a flashback of being carried on a litter to a helicopter, and then I passed out again.

I woke up with a saline IV in my arm and everything out of focus, then I passed out again. When I woke up 3 days later the doctor said that it was a close call, that I was completely dehydrated, and that body parts were starting to shut down. I was ordered to stay put, rest, and drink a lot of water. After a week and a half in the mash unit, they discharged me, and I hitched a ride back to the CP in Dong Ha where I reported to the top sergeant. After dressing me down for being stupid, he actually said I did okay to make it as far up the hill as I did, but in the future I should have a medic check me out if I am not feeling well.

I know you are worrying about me, but be assured I'm okay. I made it past near miss #8!

Love, George

Dear Mom and Dad, 8/3/66

Well, I'm back at camp and certified ready for combat. The first thing I wanted to know was what happened with Hastings, so I asked one of the radio operators what he knew. I could only imagine the horror of what happened to our men, some of whom were friends. His eyes started brimming with tears as he gave me an emotional account of the events. After I was removed from the hill, apparently all hell broke loose. Several CH-46 Sea Knight helicopters were shot down or crashed with troops on board. While trying to escape the choppers, some of the Marines were killed by the blades, and some were injured by the crash. Our ground troops could see the Sea Knights in flames trying to land. They could see men, some on fire, jumping off, preferring their chances of survival from injuries to burning alive in a crashed chopper. But the NVA was firing on the downed CH-46s and killing or wounding more Marines.

I also learned that later that day an air strike was called in by our radio operator to support Marines who were pinned down by the VC in the valley below the CP. Due to misinterpreted coordinates, an F-4 Phantom came roaring in over our CP and fired two missiles directly into the middle of our camp instead of the valley. Someone managed to radio the Phantom to call off the strike before it came back again. This all took place where I most likely would have been with my radio had I made this operation. I probably would have been injured or killed, so I guess that is near miss #9, and my luck is still holding. We do a lot of praying these days, especially for our guys who were wounded, and we were thankful to hear no one was killed.

I was searching for my friend Paul when the sergeant told me that he was wounded in the left arm by shrapnel on July 24th during the operation and was sent to the hospital ship to recover. I'm waiting to hear of his condition and hoping he is okay.

I can only imagine how this is affecting everyone at home, but hang in there because I plan to be okay.
Love, George

Operation Hastings is also known as Helicopter Valley. The operation was a combined effort of our military and the ARVIN to push back NVA regiments that had crossed the DMZ and were threatening to attack and liberate Quang Tri Province in South Vietnam. On July 15, 1966, the 3rd Battalion, 4th Marines, were being transported to Landing Zone (LZ) Crow about five miles north of the Rockpile. I knew back then I had to find out more about Hastings and include what happened if I ever wrote a book about Nam. I found the following article online at the Vietnam Helicopter Pilots Association website (vhpa.org). I received approval to use this article in its entirety.

"how 'Helicopter Valley' got its name information"
for HMM-164
HMM-265
MAG-16
Helicopter Valley
For date 660715

HMM-164 was a US Marine Corps unit
HMM-265 was a US Marine Corps unit
MAG-16 was a US Marine Corps unit
Primary service involved, US Marine Corps
South Vietnam
Description: After Marine jets and artillery prepped to two initial assault LZs for operation HASTINGS, 24 CH-46s from HMM-164 and HMM-265 brought the first wave of Marines from 3rd Battalion, 4th Marines into LZ Crow, about five miles northeast of the Rockpile starting at 0800. The 24 CH-46As were divided into six divisions of four aircraft each since LZ Crow appeared large enough to accommodate four aircraft landing together. Each

CH-46 carried 14 troops plus a crew of four. Since numerous automatic weapon positions were located to the northeast, the final approach heading was generally southeast, which caused the terrain to slope downhill to the zone. There was a tailwind of about 5 knots. The first two divisions landed in Crow without incident. HMM-265's EP-155, in the third division, overshot the landing point and hit a tree line, causing strike damage plus minor injuries to the crew and passengers. It came to rest to the right, outside and [sic] the zone and was smoking. HMM-164's YT-15, flown by MAJ Tom Reap, was the fifth division leader. The second ship in the fifth division was HMM-164's YT-18, flown by CPT W.J. Sellers. HMM-265's EP-160, flown by CPT R.O. Harper, was the third ship and CPT L. Farrell in EP-174 was the last ship in the fifth division which approached the zone in a free-trail formation. In the report of aircraft mishap, MAJ Reap stated he believed he was slightly high and fast on final. Rather than flare and place his wingman in an awkward position, he picked a clear area about 75 feet east of the LZ. He came to a hover and the crew helped him avoid a small ridge already occupied by Marines. He started losing rotor RPM as he pulled power to move over the ridge. The CH-46 dropped the last 8–10 feet to the ground and landed hard. Sellers was about four rotor diameters behind Reap and a little higher. He flared to about 20 degrees nose up to get rid of this airspeed and moved abeam of the leader as he came to a high hover. Some trees near the stream, a stand of 20 foot bamboo, and troops already on the ground limited his touchdown choices. He started losing RPM in the hover and set down to the left of Reap. Both CH-46s were on uneven ground. YT-18 was only on the ground about four seconds before it meshed aft rotors with YT-15, which had already lowered its ramp and troops were leaving. Both aircraft began to shake and vibrate violently; then broke at the splice just forward of the aft pylon. The pylon dropped, injuring some men inside. YT-15's blades killed two Marines who had just left the aircraft. At 1815, while inserting a reaction company to guard the three CH-46s in LZ Crow, HMM-265's EP-171, flown by CPT T.C. McAllister with SGT R.R. Telfer as crew chief, was hit at 1,500 feet by 12.7 mm fire. Photos taken from the ground show smoke coming from the cockpit windows and flames from the rear of the aircraft. When they tried landing on Crow, smoke filled the cockpit so no one could see. They overshot the LZ and crashed on the edge of the battalion's CP and 81 mortars. Thirteen Marines died and three were injured in this incident. Thereafter, the Marines referred to the Ngan River Valley as "Helicopter Valley."[1]

While writing this book, I was able to obtain several letters that my friend Paul sent home when he was wounded, commenting on the war and his personal feelings about his injury and Operation Hastings. My letters, which tell of actual events, were never sent home, while Paul's were sent and received by his family, and later they were given to me. He returned to our battalion on August 5. Following are Paul's letters sent home. For reference, when Paul mentions TM, she is Paul's younger sister Theresa Marie. Margaret was his girlfriend from Fayetteville, North Carolina, and Jack was his brother from Roanoke.

July 25, 1966
Hi Everybody,
   Last night the "Charlie" hit us with 82 mm mortars and caused quite a few casualties. I was hit by shrapnel in the upper left arm. Right now I am on the hospital ship Repose. I'm all right so there is no need to worry. Tomorrow they are going to cut the junk out of my arm, and I should be back with my men within two or three weeks. We were lucky—I was the only radioman hit. We have been doing some hard fighting up north, and they are still at it this morning. I hope they can fight their way out of there. It's real rough. In a way I'm glad to be out of there, but I hope I can get back soon. That's a darn good battalion.
   I just wrote to Margaret and told her I was OK. She'll probably worry as much as you. Tell Jack that this ship is really living. Plenty of water, Navy nurses, and fresh chow. I guess that's how the Army lives all the time.
   Here comes the nurse with my Demerol. I have to close for now. That stuff puts me on cloud 9. Really, I'll be OK. Don't worry.
Paul
P.S. This stuff is better than beer.

July 27, 1966
Hello Everybody,
   Yesterday they took out a piece of iron from my arm that was about the size of a piece of gravel. They left the rest in and said that it wouldn't bother me. Already the holes are starting to heal, and the bleeding has stopped. There is no infection, and I am looking forward to going back to 2/4 sometime around the 2nd or 3rd of August. My main concern is that I have no clothes here. They say they'll give them to me just before I leave.
   The ship is fairly large and is the cleanest I have ever been on. There is fresh chow and plenty of fresh, clean water to drink. We can take all the showers we like, and believe me, the head is always full. There is a PX and a snack bar. Believe it or not I just don't see a thing I want. I have lost my taste for candy and things like that. I'll be crying for them when I get ashore probably.
   Funny thing about getting hit. You always hear that you don't feel a thing, but you never really believe it. It's true. You continue talking on the radio and never know what happens. Then you look down at raw flesh hanging on your arm, pull out a bandage, tie it on, and continue your work. It's hard to believe until it actually happens.
   Now a little about the Operation Hastings. There were six battalions of Marines out there in the jungle-covered mountains. We were the strike force and were the first in. My Company "E" was the first on the ground. There was very little water except what we caught in our ponchos, and it was extremely hot. We were so close to NVA

that you could yell across the border. We never crossed it. Our initial landing was on the 15th of July right after we left Da Nang.

The first couple of days we were OK all in all, and everyone was in good spirits. On the 17 our sister bn., 3/4 was trapped by the NVA regulars in a valley about five miles to our east. We fought our way up the valley never leaving the river and got to their position. There were bodies everywhere, and the water was no good to drink. It took us two full days and one night to get through this area. I was lucky because not one of my men or radios was hurt. We communicated extremely well. We took light casualties and were very tired when we reached K Co. 3/4. One man is still alive from that company. Only one.

We buried our dead and blew up everything we couldn't carry. Choppers couldn't get to us because of the heavy fire from Russian-made 12.7 mm antiaircraft gun emplacements. We tried to take as many bodies as we could, but there were too many. That is the first time we ever left a dead man behind, and it hurt each and every one of us. Some men went crazy and went running into the jungle firing and throwing grenades. Many VC were killed this way.

We all pulled back to a high land plateau where we evacuated all the wounded and received supplies. We never received a single replacement until the night I left. After a three-day rest General English CIC Delta Task Force ordered 2/4 to take and hold the valley we had just left.

Together with Golf and Hotel Co we moved back into the valley. The bodies we saw before were now bloated, covered with maggots, and some were just bare bones. Complete decay in 3 days is normal in the jungle. We moved easily and without opposition up the valley till we reached the head of it where you are surrounded by hills and are easy prey for VC snipers. Hotel moved in first and killed two and wounded six. We went next and lost the Captain, the new Lieutenant, and a good friend of mine who was Platoon Sargent. Golf moved in with no resistance. We formed up in a 360° perimeter for the night and rested. The next day we started to call in close air support from Marine planes on carriers offshore. This was to prove to be a mistake. Along with a Captain from the air wing as an advisor, my men brought them in underground radio control. He was the one who gave them their target in Pilot lingo. The plane, an A & D Fantom, came in on a heading of 340° magnetic over the hills, and directly over our position he dropped two 250 lb. bombs. I was about 20 yds away and in a foxhole. They looked like they were coming down my throat. My friend and I escaped uninjured, but there were five casualties all of which were very minor. This I contribute to a miracle and a lot of quick prayers. All air support was then called off, and we used 155 mm artillery which did an extremely good job as far as we could tell.

The next day was very quiet, and we only had 2 killed. In the afternoon it rained so hard that you couldn't hear yourself talk. That's when "Charlie" moved his 82 mm mortar into position and waited. It was about 1800 when we started to settle down for the night. People were bailing out their foxholes and cleaning up from the rain. We never finished cleaning our radios that night.

The first round hit the center of the perimeter, and the rest hit all around. They have a strange, deep, heavy sound, those 82 mm's. Deadly is the only word to describe it.

After all was over we ordered an emergency resupply of ammo. We were very short by this time. It was on a supply chopper that I made it out of there and to the field hospital at Dong Ha. From there I was sent directly here, and the rest you know. That is how it was, only it was much worse than it appeared to us who were there. People here are used to death and the smell of bodies in the sun. Men here are men from 18 years and up. They are men.

On my 21st birthday I legally became of age, but I know myself that it was in 1965 when I was first shot at. Hasting will never be forgotten by those who were in it. Each man can tell the story to someone who was not there, but it will have little meaning to them just as it is a story from far away to you. Those of us who were there, who bled there, and who died violently there will be forgotten in a few weeks by the public but not by each other. That "Valley of Death" will haunt many dreams for many years to come.

This letter may shock you but every word is true, and there are many details left out because I don't wish to write a book. That's how it was and still is for the men out there. Maybe they'll go to Heaven, maybe Hell. Whichever place we go, we'll be together. The Corp's hymn says that the streets of heaven are guarded by Marines. I sincerely hope so. They deserve it more than any others.

One day I may write a book about this. I hope I am given the chance. I'll write again soon. Tell TM to light a candle for all of us. We need it.
Paul

August 2, 1966
Hi Everyone,

I am still on this miserable ship, and the way things look I'll be here another 8–9 days. I feel very good, and my arm doesn't bother me at all. They just won't let you off until you are in perfect shape. What a waste of people.

We pulled into the Da Nang harbor this morning and we'll probably be here for a few days. This would be a good time for all aboard to go to the Army club and get drunk, but they say we are too sick or too weak to go. I'll tell you one thing. If they ever let us go now we would tear the place down. The Army didn't lose one man on Hastings.

I haven't received any mail for over a month now except for the birthday cards. I guess it is piling up in some off-the-wall place here in VN (Vietnam). I wouldn't mind a letter or two now and then. Down with all mailmen. They get their mail and to hell with the guys who aren't around. When I get back to 2/4 you can bet I'll raise hell about this. I'll probably make L/cpl.

Some three-star general is running around here today telling everyone how proud he is of us. That guy is the biggest bag of wind I've ever seen. If we're so darn great, why don't they give us a leave or let us out of here. Words are cheap here on the Repose especially if you're a general. Who cares about him? All I want to do is go back and get a company again.

We got the word that there is another operation going on and that 2/4 has moved to Dong Ha permanently. It seems like they'll never give them a rest. 1/4 hasn't been on an operation for 7 months. They sit and guard the supplies. They have more men than 2/4 & 3/4 combined. Somebody must have something on somebody to keep them out of the field. If they ever do go out they'll probably all get killed because they have no experience.

What is Jack doing for a living? I wonder what it's like to be a civilian. Must be great. I guess TM is getting ready to go back to school soon and is glad to have Jack home. Do they fight all the time? Since I've been here I've read four books and still have time left to goof off. It's bad when you have to try to be lazy. It's time for chow so I'll close for now. Say hello to all those people around Roanoke for me and tell the <u>Marine Recruiter to go to hell</u>.
P.M.

August 4, 1966
Hi Everybody,

Today was a rather big day here aboard the Repose. The two generals from the Marine Divisions here in Vietnam came out to give us our Purple Hearts. For a change the generals catered to us troops and held a very informal ceremony. Along with a little speech and a lot of handshaking came our medals. If I can, I'll mail it to you along with one of the pieces of metal removed from my arm. Don't lose it. I'd hate to have to get another one to replace it. When I get back to 2/4 I have another medal to send home. The Good Conduct for successfully getting away with all kinds of underhanded things. If they'll give me my other two medals I can call it even. I don't want any more. Not until I get a few days leave in at least.

From what I can find out from the doctor I will be here about six more days. By that time they'll have to stick me in the nut ward. There is no action on ship. Routine is no good after four months fighting "Charlie." What I need is a great big drink, about a three-day leave on some beach somewhere with no one to bother me, and plenty of people to fight with. Maybe Jack's & TM could drink my beer for me. TM should be able to outdrink Jack. How about it, Sissy?

I haven't been paid since sometime in June I think. The last time was when I sent the check home. My funds are running low now, and I hope they'll pay me soon. I'll send enough home to finish off the car and put a little more into savings. I think the checking account should be doing all right. Send me a statement on it.

Speaking of money, I have an account with the Marine Credit Union at Lejeune. If anything happens to me there is some money there. They are getting $25 a month and pay very good interest. I don't know how much is there now.

Still haven't received any mail at all. I'll have a big bundle when I get back to 2/4. Did I tell you that the battalion has moved up to Dong Ha—our new home. It's so very close to the border. There'll be a lot of action there. I'll be glad to get back.

Guess it's time to close for now. Time to take a shower and go to the movie. Another benefit of the Navy. See you later.
PM

OPERATION PRAIRIE 11

The NVA offered 700 American dollars as a bounty to any of their men who killed a radio operator or officer. Being assigned to a rifle squad or platoon meant certain contact with the enemy, so the radio operators would be the target of choice for snipers. We were just resting and waiting to hear when the next operation would start. With nothing else to occupy our minds except thoughts of our next mission, we were extremely concerned that, due to injuries and death from our last operation, we were short of operators. This meant officers or one of the men would have to assume that role, taking them away from their duties. And personally, we were all conscious of the reality that we were targets with a price on our heads.

Dear Mom and Dad,   8/6/66
My friend Paul just returned from the hospital ship fully recovered from his wound from Operation Hastings. It was a huge relief when we heard that he was okay and see him back in our battalion. I could tell he was glad to be off that ship. We talked about Hastings and what happened to 3rd Battalion, 4th Marines, in Helicopter Valley. No one should have to live through what Paul and those men went through that day. His grief and anger, as he spoke, were so palpable, and his description was so shockingly vivid that I could almost hear the screams and smell the fuel as the choppers went up in flames. I could taste bile rising to my throat and feel the profound grief of watching men tangled in chopper blades or jumping to their death. Tears come every time I think of it, and my dreams are getting worse.

I told Paul about my heatstroke and what had happened to me on the first day that landed me in the field hospital. I don't know how to reconcile my feelings about being carried out before all hell broke loose. It is a strange mixture of guilt that I was lucky enough to get out of there, even though I came close to dying myself, and of relief that I made it out. I guess we're both feeling pretty lucky to be alive.

One night after chow, Paul and I were having a few warm beers in his hooch, talking about our families. I told Paul that I have two sisters and five nephews and that you both had hoped for a granddaughter but got five grandsons instead. Guess I have to be the one to have the girl for them if I am lucky enough to make it out of this mess. After downing a couple of six packs, we starting joking around and got pretty morbid about not making it home alive. He told me I would be blown up and scattered over Nam, and I told him that he would be carried out in a body bag. I think it was our way of dumping our anxiety, but it got weird and morbid, so we changed the subject to cars pretty quickly.

It was getting late, and the beer was gone, but before leaving, Paul and I made a promise to each other that if one of us didn't make it home the other would visit family and deliver a message of his last thoughts of them. I'm sorry, Mom and Dad, that this is so heavy and not what parents want to hear in letters home, but I'd like you to know that all we all think about is our families and want to somehow send comfort if the worst happens.

Someone once said that soldiers should think of each other as military acquaintances only and not friends because when critical decisions need to be made, there can be no hesitations. We can't let personal feelings for others influence actions that might save or jeopardize the whole company. But we feel like brothers, and our friendship and passing time together helps take our minds off the war. It's meant everything to have someone here while we're so far from home and to feel I've got Paul's back and he's got mine.

The battalion sometimes offers a religious service before an operation for anyone who cares to attend. Last Sunday a priest gave an all-denomination service. I haven't been to church for a long time, so I went and prayed for our battalion and for safety in the next operation. They say there are no atheists in the foxhole. I don't know about that, but I know it made me feel better to believe we weren't alone and someone was watching over us. Attending worship brought back memories of our church—Dad in your suit and tie, and Mom all dressed up with her Easter hat. I also remember that by the sermon I would be dozing off until the closing hymn. I didn't sleep this time.

Have to go and hopefully get a good night's sleep without nightmares. Please pray for me.
Love, George

Dear Mom and Dad,   *9/1/66*
Operation Hastings was followed by Operation Prairie. Our battalion was on the move again from Dong Ha to support Operation Prairie near the DMZ. Our mission was to search for NVA, engage, and destroy.

It was already promising to be a hot one when our battalion left Dong Ha late morning with our company leading the way to a suspected NVA stronghold in a mountain known as the Rockpile. The mountain had caves and interconnecting tunnels used by the NVA as a CP and hiding place. It seemed like we were marching forever, but finally we arrived at the observation hill near the Rockpile and set up our CP. After we made camp, we started to dig the shallow foxholes, our only protection. Paul was the assigned field radio operator for his company and went out with them to search the Rockpile for reported NVA. I was one of several radio operators working in the CP for the colonel. As Paul's company approached the base of the mountain, they stopped for a short break. Little did they know the mountain was crawling with NVA who were positioned in the caves looking down at the company through the crosshairs of their weapons.

Back at the CP, we suddenly heard the sounds of M14s & M79s being fired. I was on the radio when the fighting started, and I could hear the commotion, gunshots, and screaming on the phone. We could hear the other operators shouting they were under attack and needed support. Over my radio I recognized Paul's voice saying he was hurt, and he was asking for help. I was desperate to get to Paul and help him and his men when I saw a rifle team forming to rescue Paul's company. Grabbing my rifle and some ammo, I ran to join the relief team, but the top sergeant stopped me and refused to let me go. We were still short of radio operators, and I was needed at the CP. I said I was going to help Paul's company and argued with him to let me go, but he commanded me to stay and I had no choice. You should know that under wartime conditions, disobeying an order could mean facing a firing squad or prison. Ten or twenty minutes went by when I finally got permission to join the relief team if they were still in sight. I collected all my equipment and ran to the slope of our hill, but by then they were long gone and I couldn't catch up. I was shaking with anger and worry, but there was nothing I could do but return to my radio watch on the hill.

Throughout the night we continued to hear Paul asking for help. The relief team was able to get close to Paul's position, but they were pinned down by the enemy fire and snipers. Another radio operator in the relief team, William (Bill) Wright, a former policeman from NY, took charge and called in artillery on the Rockpile, but he was not able to get to Paul's company. Throughout the night we continued to hear Paul asking for help, but we could do nothing, and the battle went on with Bill calling in more artillery fire. I was beside myself with fear and terrified for them. I felt so helpless, and I know I will never forget those voices on the radio and Paul calling to us. They had a few firefights during the night, and Paul stayed on the radio giving the NVA locations that he could see. By early morning his radio was silent and he didn't answer my calls, but I could hear his voice in my head calling for help and I was sick with helplessness and hopelessness.

The morning brought more gunfire and explosions. The NVA was all over our Marines and gaining ground. So far our artillery was not effective, and it appeared that many Marines would be wounded or killed. The radio operator from the relief team, Bill Wright, called in a fire mission of 105 howitzers. The first rounds exploded within the perimeter of Bill's team. They asked Bill if he wanted to adjust the rounds away from his men, but he said to "fire for effect" in the same coordinates where he and his men were taking cover.

As rounds of artillery continued to hit the area with explosions sending shrapnel everywhere, he told his men to get low and hug the ground. They were being overrun by the NVA, and the only choice for Bill was to call in the artillery bombardment on his position. Our artillery was on target, and finally the NVA retreated. By some miracle a few men were wounded, but most survived. Later that morning Bill's team cleared the mountain of NVA and recovered our dead and wounded who were medevacked out. When the men came back and told me Paul was killed in the early morning by a gunshot to the head, I remember dropping to the ground stunned, feeling like I would be sick. Sitting there in utter disbelief, I had the overwhelming feeling that I failed to help my friend and it cost him his life, and I had no idea what to do with the feelings that were assaulting me. Only a short time ago we'd gotten drunk together and joked about who wouldn't make it back, as if by joking we could keep the inconceivable from happening. That night, after three days in hell that changed the lives of so many people, including mine, we left the Rockpile and made our way back to camp. I was empty of emotion, exhausted, and depressed.

Paul never abandoned his radio. He was able to let us know what was happening on the ground and what the enemy was up to. Because of his unbridled heroism and amazing acts of courage, many lives were saved. Through all the pandemonium and terror of that battle—the enemy gunfire, deafening explosions, and specters of VC surrounding him—Paul stayed till the end to save others. And I want to tell the world that Paul was—is—a hero of the highest degree. And Bill Wright deserves our highest honor for his heroism and actions that also saved many lives that day.

I can't believe how naive I was about what it means to be in a war, and for the first time it isn't just someone else's war in a faraway country. It feels very personal now, and I know I'll never be the same person that I was when I enlisted. I just want to come home and put all of this behind me. I miss all of you so much and I love you.
George

Dear Mom and Dad,   10/15/66
It's been 53 days since Paul died. Imagine that, 53 days—less than 2 months ago and the lives of the people who knew and loved Paul are forever changed. I can't bring myself to think of how his family is coping with their loss. Their suffering is beyond my imagination, and I am ashamed that all I can do is try not to think about it.

Funny thing, war. One day you are alive, and the next day you are gone. Yet life goes on and we're expected to get back to work as usual as though hell hadn't erupted everywhere with men smack in the middle of the madness and mayhem. As though they hadn't called out helplessly, endlessly for the aid that wouldn't come on time before they were struck down and gone. As though they hadn't known their fate as fear overwhelmed their senses. And yet they still performed their job that was drilled into them for so many months, the job that made them heroes. Dead ones.

I've been walking around in a daze, numb to the world that now has no meaning, or color, or beauty in the God-forsaken jungle. Some days I'm overcome with rage and the overwhelming need to pummel something into oblivion until complete exhaustion gives way to blessed sleep. Sleep without the same deadly dream that haunts my nights and occupies my days as I find myself replaying it over and over, screen by screen, like a movie that I could cut and splice out the deadly scenes to make the outcome different.

Last night I dreamed I was swimming in a puddle with the baby rats. As I watched them struggle to get to safe ground, I felt the water cover my head. The harder I tried to swim, the farther away it seemed, and I couldn't quite make it. It probably sounds crazy, but I even keep thinking back to when I was tempted to save the baby rats. Now every time I see one, I'm seeing VC, and I don't care if they drown because they are our enemy, and I want to kill every one of them! I feel like reality is slipping away and I'm going under too.

I'm so sorry, Mom & Dad, to pour out my guts like this in a letter. But I don't know who else to tell. I just need to get it out of my head, and I don't know how. The silence among the men is deafening. I know they feel the same way, but no one talks about it. The good news is our battalion may go back to Okinawa to regroup and get some much-needed R & R. But first the gunny just told us to get ready for some field training in Da Nang. Try not to worry. I really will be okay, and I'll write again soon. With much love, George

Looking back, we were unaware of the strategic importance Operations Hastings and Prairie played in the Vietnam War. The NVA had, for some time, been infiltrating south of the DMZ with the mission of securing a foothold in some of the key towns of South Vietnam in the Quang Tri Province. If allowed or unchallenged, the buildup would cost more lives in the future to take back these towns. The NVA was pushed back to the DMZ in Operation Hastings during July, but they had regrouped and were on the move back to South Vietnam again, and we had to stop them.

Operation Hastings ended August 3, 1966. Operation Prairie started August 3, 1966, and ended on October 27, 1966. Most of the contact with the NVA was around Mutter's Ridge, the Razorback, and the Rockpile.[1] As grunts, rarely informed of the bigger picture, we only concerned ourselves with carrying out our mission and staying alive. The cost for this mission was incredibly high. The sacrifice Paul and so many others made during these operations still makes me question the war, and I constantly think, why the others and not me? Why did I get back in one piece? Whenever I attended a function, family or otherwise, I would think, I am doing all the things that Paul will not be doing, and I still feel deep sadness for all the "might have been" that Paul will never experience.

Paul Reed was awarded the Silver Star for heroism. While fatally wounded, he managed to stay on his radio and continue giving out enemy positions until his final breath.

Bill Wright was also awarded the Silver Star for his heroism in Operation Prairie. By his selfless and brave act of directing artillery on his own position to push back the NVA, many lives were saved.

Recently I was in contact with Bill, and we talked for hours over the phone and got reacquainted. After the war he joined the New York Police Department from which he retired, and he is still living in New York. Bill said he always wanted to write about his time in Nam but never got around to it, so he gave me some stories to include in my book. The following commentary is the story, as told to me by Bill during our phone interview in 2014, of what he experienced during the night and day at the Rockpile when his platoon tried to save Paul's company. I have tried to convey this as accurately as possible.

As we approached the Rockpile, the NVA opened fire, and we started to take casualties. I immediately called in for air support while taking charge of the situation. The NVA had us pinned down, and they were on the move to infiltrate and attack our position while shooting down from the Rock. We kept a constant barrage of air strikes and artillery on the Rock and close to our position. We had engaged the NVA with everything we had. It seemed like they were surrounding us, and it was getting close to hand-to-hand combat.

At dusk the fighting slowed down, and we knew they would be resting and regrouping the same as we were. Paul had been separated from his company and was closer to the base of the Rock. I heard his cries for help on the radio but could not get to him. I made the decision to go out and recon the area myself to see if I could find any NVA asleep or not alert and take them out. I hugged the ground and crawled into the black abyss where I came upon three NVA soldiers in an open area. It looked like they were asleep, and I pulled out my Ka-Bar (military knife) and slowly moved toward them. I knew if I made the slightest sound they would wake up, and I would be fighting for my life against three men.

The first man seemed to be sound asleep, so I got as close to him as I could without waking him. My plan was to cut the throat of the first man while moving onto the second. My fear was the third man would wake up and we would be doing hand-to-hand combat. I made my move and got the first man, rolled over, and got the second man. The third man was startled, and that gave me time to jump him and stab him. He put up a hard fight, and it took ten or fifteen stabs to kill him; then I pulled back and moved into the brush to wait for a time I could rejoin my company. While waiting, I heard the gurgling sound of the men whose throats I had cut. This went on for a few minutes that seemed like forever, and the sound was getting to me. Finally it grew faint, and I was relieved to be able to crawl back to my men.

The morning brought back an intense attack by the NVA, from the Rock and from the ground. Our chances of survival were slim, so I called an artillery strike on my position. I told the men to get down, hug the ground, and say a prayer. The ground moved, rocks and boulders from the Rock all hit us at one time, and I believed we were on our way to meet our Maker. The Fire Direction Center asked if I wanted more rounds to the same coordinates, and I said to fire for effect and keep them coming. I finally called off the artillery and checked the area for NVA, and they were gone. Men were wounded and dying, and I called our CP and told them to get medevac choppers in ASAP. We found Paul's body, and it appeared that he was shot in the head in the morning by one of the retreating NVA. He still had his radio handset in his hand.

I have many bad dreams about Vietnam. The demons are at work and won't leave me alone. It's hard to talk about this and keep my head from stirring up these memories.

I had sent Bill a draft of Operation Prairie from our first interview that describes what happened when Paul's company engaged the NVA. Bill's extraction company was pinned down trying to get to Paul's company. Bill wanted to clarify some of my recollection of the events that took place that day on the front lines. Following are his comments:

George, I did a little investigation after our last conversation and wondered why the Hotel Company commander put his whole company on the front line. He did not move up to the Rockpile. He moved up to the Razorback Mountain, which is opposite of the Rockpile.

They assigned me to Fox Company as tactical air control chief. We departed Dong Ha for Operation Prairie. We landed near the Razorback Mountain in two H-34 helicopters just as it was going dark. The captain sent down a rat patrol of 12 ARVIN to scout the area, and they came under fire. They were pinned down, and we had no supporting arms to help them. We were out of range of an artillery. They threw us in there like meat hooks. We were "snuffies." That term was used for me in my first combat situation down in Da Nang when the company captain there said, "Send some snuffies up here." I thought it was a new weapon. I was a lance corporal then. I said, "Thank God!" "Oh my God," I said to the sergeant. "Where is the snuffie? What is it?" He said, "That's you. Get up there." That's what the captain called snuffies.

We didn't even have two Phantoms (F-4 fighter jets). Normally we had two Phantoms on deck. The pilot would call down and say, "Low on fuel, give us targets of opportunity." They didn't even have that support to give us! Later that night, the helicopters finally brought in two 106 recoilless rifles for supporting arms. I thought, "How the hell did we even get in this place?" The NVA was threatening to overrun our company, so I was calling in the 106 shellings on our location to stop the NVA.

George, do you know they put us right in the middle of three NVA regiments—right on the DMZ—with no supporting arms? I didn't even think about the three guys I killed. I had stumbled upon them when one of the 106 rounds went off, hit the trees, and several of our guys were wounded.

Sometimes I think, "Did all these guys die for nothing? What was it for? What the hell was it for?" Who are you going to vote for, George? It almost makes me cry. Every night I cannot sleep. I just don't want to be in this world anymore! Something is coming, I can feel it.

Bill is one of our heroes, and so are the others who fight the fight every day. God bless you, my brother.

Of all the chapters in this book, this one was the hardest to write. I have kept Paul's memory alive for over 50 years, and writing this transported me back to that time and place and those events. Once again, I found myself in the emotional state I was in when Paul died. I hear his last words calling out for help on the radio. I see his face as clearly as the picture in this book. I relive our times together and hear his voice and his easy laughter. I see his warm smile and remember how bright and funny he was and remember again why we became such good friends. Now Paul is forever young and truly missed. Recently I visited the Vietnam Memorial and touched Paul's name, my last physical connection to him, profoundly sad, and one that I will always remember.

SUZUKI   12

Dear Mom and Dad,   *10/20/66*
I just completed a demolition training course in Da Nang called Land Mine Warfare and Demolitions School conducted by the 3rd Engineering Battalion. We learned how to use explosives to blow up trees and bridges with detonation cord and C4 (pliable high explosives). The detonation cord is also a high explosive, so if you wrap it around something and knot it, the cord will explode. The extent of explosion is equal to the amount of the cord turns and knots. They also showed us how to set up the M16 "Bouncing Betty" or "Jumping Jack" land mine. Unfortunately, once set up, the mine cannot be disabled, and it must be detonated with a C4 charge. One of the most important rules when working with high explosives is to do it yourself because a mistake can be fatal. We learned that both Americans and VC use these mines as traps to cause casualties.

They showed us the mousetrap, a handy little device that is sensitive to weight. It is small enough to place under a piece of chocolate in a box of candy so when the chocolate is removed from the box, the drop in weight will set off the mousetrap and high explosives under the box. It is enough to take out a complete room. I'm not sure how I'll use this in my future, but maybe I can blow up that old tree stump in the backyard when I get home.

Write soon.
Love, George
P.S. Will you please let me know if you are receiving my hazardous duty pay every month? I should have enough to buy a car when I get home.

Note: The M16 land mine is buried in the ground so that when it is stepped on, a charge launches the mine one to two meters into the air. A second charge ignites the main charge, sending fragments 360 degrees, covering a one-hundred-meter radius.[1]

Three years of military life had passed, and I was on the downhill side of my enlistment. During that time, I never had a girlfriend, and I had to admit that between missing family and having no feminine company, I was pretty lonely. Some guys still had a girl back home waiting, and others did meet girls and had relationships, but the constant traveling to Europe, the Caribbean, Asia, and back really made it difficult. Most of us settled for barhopping and one-night stands. I admit that what I dreamed about was having someone waiting back home—someone to write to and look forward to seeing when I finally stepped off that plane for good. By now I had lost contact with my friends at home, most of whom had moved on with their lives, and my old girlfriend had gotten married, so other than family, there was no one special to think about and look forward to seeing.

Dear Mom and Dad,   *11/7/66*
I'm writing from Okinawa where our battalion was sent to regroup and get some rest and relaxation (R & R). We were so excited when we received the news and couldn't wait to leave Nam and see the skies of Japan. After 6 long months in that hellhole, we were charged up with the anticipation of decent food and an actual good night's sleep. What I really wish is that I could come home and see family and find old friends, but right now I will settle for Japan.

We were driven to the Da Nang airport in transport trucks and once again herded off and into a C-130 cargo plane for the trip to Kadena Airport, Okinawa. As the backdoor closed and Nam faded into the distance, I was vaguely aware of leaving behind the constant fear of capture or dying that is the center of our daily existence. The flight to Kadena was short, but I managed to sleep the entire time, confident that we were safely far from surprise attacks on our CP. From there we were transported to the Marine Corps camp and arrived late that night to our barracks. I went straight to bed, thinking about the breakfast I would devour in the morning. As I drifted off with the smell of the clean sheets cradling me, I had a vague feeling of home. In the morning I realized, Mom, how much clean sheets could mean, and how much I took for granted all that you do to make my life comfortable. Thanks so much!

That's it for now. Would you mind sending cash and cigarettes?
Love, George

Dear Mom and Dad,   *11/25/66*
My second day in Okinawa was a disappointment. I got up early in the morning, put on my khaki uniform, grabbed all my cash, and headed for the doors to freedom. Unfortunately, I didn't get very far. I was stopped at the door by the top sergeant, and he told me that they needed to pull some men to help relieve the guards at a radar installation that monitors air traffic incoming to Kadena that was located on the top of a mountain several hours from our camp. I could not believe this—instead of the promised R & R, I would be stuck on a mountain guarding some radar installation!

The sergeant said it would only be for 2–3 days, so I put on my old utility greens and joined the rest of our unhappy bunch for the truck ride.

We arrived in the afternoon and found our way to the tent that would be our new home. Actually, the duty wasn't bad. We just ate, slept, and played cards for the most part. The three days passed quickly enough, and we got orders to grab the next truck heading out back to our barracks. Since I missed R & R, they gave me a week off, and I wasted no time getting into my khakis and running for a cab (or takushi) and instructed the driver to take me around the island.

I saw some towns that were amazingly beautiful and others that still looked like they did during WWII after the occupation of Okinawa and Japan. Many homes were still leveled, and there was barbed-wire fencing. In some areas it seems time has stood still. The buildings still standing have distinctive Japanese architectural detailing with red tile roofs, traditional front deck, and sliding doors. Japan impresses me as a culture that has a plan for everything, and everything has a relationship to each other. I especially liked the ponds and gardens that are so well designed. I think you guys would love this place.

The taxi stopped in a small town near Naha (the capitol of Okinawa) on the west side of the island; I said good-bye to the cab driver and started walking the streets. The town had so many advertising signs you could not see the yellow and gray buildings. Strolling down one of the streets, I discovered several slot-car racing parlors and pachinko arcades. The pachinko game is similar to our pinball machines except you shoot a ball that falls vertically through metal pins into a hole. If you're lucky, the ball drops into a hole that gives back more balls, which you can trade in for a gift. I played for hours and broke even.

It was getting late, so I grabbed a cab to Naha in search of dinner. Taking the suggestion of some Marines I encountered earlier, I wandered into a nearby restaurant where I was escorted to a table and handed a menu that was written in Japanese. With some help from the waitress (a beautiful Japanese girl in a blue kimono), I ordered the local catch of the day served in broth with herbs and traditional satsumaimo sweet potatoes. Comfortably full and ready for a beer, I paid my bill, gave the waitress a big tip, and went to the bar where I noticed an exotic young woman. To be honest, my mind was on the possibility of finding a date for the evening.

Asian girls are so different from Americans, and I was captivated with her beautiful and exotic almond eyes and long, silky black hair. Figuring I had nothing to lose, I asked if I could join her. She smiled and gestured to me to sit down. I introduced myself, and she said her name was Suzuki. Her broken English was only fair but good enough for us to communicate, and we talked for hours. I learned that she worked as a masseuse and tried not to imagine her delicate hands kneading the exhaustion from my body after long trips into the jungle. There was a strong attraction, and when she occasionally touched my arm, I admit my heart beat a little faster. It was getting late, and Suzuki had to leave. I asked her if we could meet again to tour the island, and she agreed. We parted, and I went back to my barracks, reliving the evening and anticipating the possibilities.

When we met the next morning, I was taken again with her delicate beauty. She looked like a fragile Japanese doll. We grabbed a takushi and spent the day sightseeing around Naha. As much as I enjoyed the beautiful scenery, I couldn't keep my eyes off Suzuki. The day was about as perfect as I could have imagined, wandering through the local shops, snacking on food from various markets and street vendors, and I didn't want it to end. It took some courage, but I asked her if we could find a place to spend more time together. Surprisingly, she agreed and told me we could rent a room in town for the week. This was going to be the best R & R ever!

I can imagine what you are thinking, Mom and Dad, about me staying a week with a girl, especially one I just met. When we first arrived in Okinawa, our gunnery sergeant cautioned us about the locals wanting to get married for a ticket to the States and then get divorced. But I wanted so badly to spend what time I had with her, so I guess I conveniently forgot all of that advice.

That night she introduced me to the traditional Japanese massage, which began with a bath. Handing me a yukata, which is a lightweight kimono worn to and from a bath area, she told me to remove my clothes. Seated on a chair, she began to scrub my body with soap and a loofah, and I felt the weight of months of fighting and filth leave my body and mind. After rinsing me, she led me to a deep tub of steamy water where we immersed our bodies and held each other beneath the soothing warmth until, uninhibited, Suzuki took my hand and stepped out of the tub pulling me with her. After gently drying me, she led me to a tatami mat on the floor. Working down from my neck and back, she massaged away the tension, and as I relaxed I felt the weariness of the war dissolve. Then she applied oil and, standing on my back, she continued to massage away the last of my reserve. Gently pulling her to me, our eyes locked on each other in wonder of the arousal, and I was unprepared for the velvet feeling of her skin against mine as we came together for the first time.

That night as we lay together in each other's arms, I felt passion I had never known before. None of the backseat necking or fooling around I experienced at home had prepared me for the intensity of this moment, and I just wanted to stay in that place next to Suzuki's tender body forever. I kept looking at her to make sure this was real and not some hallucination, and I tried to forget that I was heading back to the harsh reality of Nam, knowing I would relive this moment over and over. I figured if I died in Vietnam, I would die happy.

The next day, we rented a scooter and spent the day exploring Naha, the world of Suzuki. I asked her about her family and her life, but she shared very little. She said she has a young brother and sister, which reminded me of the children in Vietnam and the abandoned village where we made camp, and I wondered what kind of life and future they could look forward to. I was surprised to learn that, like many Naha residents, both of her parents work for the U.S. government. Her dad is a WW2 veteran and one of the defenders of the 1945 Battle of Okinawa, which I hadn't heard of. There was deep sadness in her eyes as she explained that nearly a third of the island's civilian population had been slaughtered. She said that he rarely mentions his military experiences, and she thinks he never really got over the horror of that war. When I asked to meet her family, she turned away and said they didn't know that she was dating an American soldier and would not have approved. "My parents would be very *disappointed in me,"* she admitted, and as much as I longed to know more about her, I understand her need to keep our relationship from them.

After a few more days of exploring and relaxation, my time was running out on my R & R, and I was determined to make the most of what we had left. As we continued to roam the island, content to simply have each other's company, it made no difference what we did. Surrounded by the extraordinary beauty of the island, I felt like I was in heaven and couldn't get enough. The ocean beckoned, and the beaches invited us to rest on the warm sand. We dove in, and waves washed over us as we dissolved into the aqua liquid and swam until we were exhausted, finally returning to our blanket. Lying side by side, we watched the sunset spreading majestic colors over the horizon until the moon revealed itself and stars twinkled above us like fireflies. It was a magical time, and I felt as though our two spirits became one.

After surviving a sake party with Suzuki's friends on our last night, we woke up late and made love. I packed my duffle bag and gazed around one last time at the room that had been our "home" for the week. Leaving my bag at the desk, we headed out to spend our final day in Naha. Walking the streets of the city, we relived our holiday week, and knowing there wasn't much chance of seeing each other again before I left for Nam, we promised to write to each other.

When the time came, I could barely let go of Suzuki. I wanted to hold on to her forever. As I gathered her sweetness into my arms one last time, I could feel her body trembling as we kissed good-bye, and I realized how vulnerable she was. Reluctantly leaving, I'm sure we were both wondering if we will ever see each other again, but I think we both knew that the reality of our separate lives and the distance between us would be too much to sustain a relationship. Returning for my bag, I left Suzuki at the room, but she stayed in my heart. My time with her was exotic and romantic and would have been unimaginable back home. I'm not sure if I was in love, but I was deeply touched and grateful for her tenderness and for our time together that, for at least a short period, made this hellish time bearable.

I've changed so much since coming here and barely remember the boy who brazenly challenged you after enlisting. All the innocence of the youthful kid that left for camp 3 years ago is gone, left somewhere in the jungle, vanished up in the smoke of napalm, and lost when Paul died. And although I know I'll never send this letter, I needed to tell you about Suzuki and what I experienced and to share it with you, at least on paper.

Thinking of you as always.
Love, George

For the first time in six months, I was able to totally leave the war behind and feel carefree again. My emotions were on a roller-coaster, but I was grateful for the time I had spent with Suzuki, and it was hard to say good-bye. And if I was lucky enough to survive and return to my life in America, so very different from the exotic world of Suzuki, I would kiss the ground and thank God every day.

As mentioned earlier, we were warned about Asian women marrying GIs to get to America. While I don't think that was the case with Suzuki, it would have been difficult to tell my Mom that I wanted to marry a Japanese girl. My Dad and the rest of my family would have been okay with it if they believed we truly loved each other, but there was so little time for that discovery. Although we exchanged addresses and promised to write, my letters went unanswered. I often wonder what happened to Suzuki and just hope she had a good life after the war with someone to love her. Thank you, Suzuki, for giving me your companionship when it was most needed and for sharing that lovely, incredible diversion from the horror across the sea to which I had to return.

Also, in my letter I mentioned that Suzuki's parents worked for the U.S. military. The Kadena Air Base in Naha, Okinawa, was a major Pentagon transport facility that served incoming and outgoing flights from the United States, Okinawa, and Vietnam. They also managed most of the fuel, ammunition, and supplies for the war effort. The people of Okinawa were deeply immersed in the war effort, with over forty thousand Okinawans employed by the military, packing explosives and doing many other jobs, including acting as the enemy in war games, for which the average pay was $1 an hour with no significant benefits. Many also worked in Okinawa fueling planes and loading ammunition, while others were employed in South Vietnam driving buses on bases or working aboard American supply ships where there were reports of Okinawans wounded and killed. The Japanese are a proud and honorable people. They suffered the worst and endured the most. Our men and women died for their democracy and right to freedom. I know that I would go back again if called, and most of my comrades would too. In 1972, Okinawa was turned over to Japan and is currently under their rule. Kadena is still a major thriving airport.

Dear Mom and Dad,   *1/5/67*
I'm still in Okinawa back at the base. Today we were trucked to a beach to rest, have some fun in the sun, and meet new replacements. I met my first American Samoan named Uinifareti Saleaumua (that's a mouthful!!) who has been assigned to our company for the redeployment back to Nam. He is friendly and pleasant, huge and strong as a bull, and not one to mess with. Saleaumua decided he would organize a Samoan cookout—which is not your typical backyard BBQ! He somehow found some chickens, which he killed, cleaned, and wrapped in banana leaves. Watching Saleaumua kill the chickens was a real shocker. He showed us how he "cranked them up" (similar to cranking an old car), which breaks their neck. Next, he dug a deep pit in the sand and lit a fire. After the wood turned to coals, he buried the chickens and covered the leaves with sand. The chickens cooked for several hours, and when he pulled them out,

we had a feast. I love your chicken, Mom, but this was totally different, and the best chicken I ever had!

When we returned to the barracks, they informed me that I had been promoted to sergeant. So . . . more rank, more responsibility, and, more important, more money! Our time here is short. I wish it was longer, and I hope someday to come back, see Okinawa again, and maybe find Suzuki.

Love, George

P.S. Would you please send some cash? I spent all my money in Okinawa and won't get my new pay raise for a couple of weeks.

Dear Mom and Dad, 1/20/67

We departed Okinawa and arrived early morning in Vietnam, landing at the Da Nang airfield, and once again we were blasted with the heat and heavy smell of fuel. We were loaded into several transport trucks, and our battalion went north to Phu Bai, our new camp location. Several replacement Marines joined our company, some with combat experience and some without. We also gained a few more, much-needed, field radio operators. I may have mentioned earlier that our radio call sign, which we use for all communication, was "Sudden Death." Our new call sign is "Ridge Beam." We preferred "Sudden Death" since it's the perfect name for what we're seeing here.

The scuttlebutt from the new guys had it that the antiwar effort was growing stronger throughout the States, especially in the colleges. This is the first I've heard any stories about the movement, with students protesting in the streets and calling soldiers baby killers. It's pretty deflating for us, considering we're supposed to be the good guys, not the bad, and still believe we are here to help build a democracy and South Vietnam independence. The Vietnamese people that we meet are mostly farmers and just want to be left alone. Unfortunately, they are caught in the crossfire between us and the Viet Cong, so they do what they have to do for their families and for survival. The VC demand food and shelter to let them live. We know old men, women, and even children are forced to lay booby traps designed to kill us. In retaliation, we are instructed by the chain of command to burn villages harboring the enemy to force them out. It's difficult to know who the enemy is, and they keep coming back! We seem to be caught in the middle of a battle with no winners. Please send me some newspaper clippings so I know what's happening back in the States. I'm not sure anymore if we are doing any good, but I've decided I won't let the protesters get me down.

Over the last few weeks, we took many trips to Da Nang for mail and to transport soldiers back and forth. I dreaded every trip, knowing the danger of land mines. It is important that everyone in the jeep look for any fresh areas of dirt on the road or mounds that could be newly planted mines. This is a common tactic of the VC, and we have to be extremely careful of the mines and of ambushes.

We're still using the old WWII leftover jeeps, which are somewhat unreliable and need a lot of maintenance to keep them running. It's not uncommon to break down and be stuck on the side of the road while we radio back for help. The good news is we just received a new Ford jeep. You know I love to drive, so I got my military driver's *certification card and volunteered to be a driver as needed now that we have something reliable.*

Yesterday the mail carrier stopped by our hooch and dumped 20–30 letters from kids at home. Apparently some high schools decided to send letters to the soldiers in Nam. The letter I got was from a senior girl with an enclosed picture. She wrote about her life in high school and said her favorite class is art. Since I've decided to attend art school after I return, I wrote back and told her my plans and that I hope she gets to pursue hers. I told her a little about life in Nam, without the gory details, and I hope she will write again. You can't imagine how much we look forward to letters from anyone at home. Those moments reading news transport us out of this hellhole for a short while and give us something else to think about and are appreciated. Speaking of letters, the military mail system has not caught up with us yet since we left from Okinawa. I miss reading your letters and hope they come soon. Won't be long now; just a few more months in the Nam, and I'll be home, God willing!

Please pray and keep writing.
Love, George

Another unspoken casualty of the war were the children born to Vietnamese women and American soldiers. While researching, I discovered several articles about Amerasians—children unwanted and often left behind to fend for themselves in the streets when their fathers returned to America. The Vietnamese people treated these orphaned children, referred to as "Children of the Dust," like dirt, with total disrespect. By the end of the war, there were thousands of these Amerasian children. Although the U.S. Defense Department did not consider them America's responsibility, in 1975 President Gerald Ford, fearing a massacre as Saigon was falling, ordered an evacuation of some two thousand children called "Operation Babylift." To everyone's great horror, the first transport plane loaded with children and staff crashed on takeoff, killing many on board. Subsequent flights were successful in transporting over three thousand more Amerasians to America, where they were placed in orphanages to be adopted by American families. We may think the war was over when the last troops departed, but the story continued for the people of Vietnam and the Children of the Dust. God bless them all.[2]

SHORT-TIMERS   13

I was getting close to end of my tour in Nam, with only a few months to go. Those of us who were rotating from Nam about the same time kept the famous short-time calendar, generally a Playboy pin-up to be truthful. We check off each day as we count down to our long-awaited joyous release from hell and return to home, that place of longing. Remember, I was told earlier that those arriving and those leaving Nam have a higher percentage of casualties due to the lack of experience or being in country too long. You can't relax until the plane lands in the States and you are once again out of harm's way. Actually, some of the short-timers were so paranoid about getting killed that they stayed in their hooch all day and only went outside for chow, bath, or radio watch in the CP. Our location at Phu Bai Combat Base was well fortified and designed to keep the enemy out, unlike in the city of Da Nang, where you could get shot just walking down the street.

Dear Mom and Dad,   *2/18/67*
I'm writing from Camp Phu Bai. I just got off radio duty and had some hot chow, so I thought I would write to you guys. We've had torrential rains for a few days, and I am sitting on my cot looking at a stream of water running directly through our hooch from one end to the other. It's so bad that the trench around our tent can't contain the rainwater, and I can't put my feet on the ground without getting soaked.

This week, one of our companies was mobilized for a mission to search out a suspected VC concentration north of Phu Bai, but I was not selected to go so I stayed back at the camp on radio duty. Saleaumua, the Samoan sergeant I mentioned earlier during my stay in Okinawa, was chosen to go with the company as one of the field radio operators and sergeant in charge. The company was gone for 2–3 days, and when they returned, one of the radio operators filled us in on their mission.

"It took most of the day, but finally by nightfall the company arrived at the suspected VC location without incident and made camp on top of a hill that provided a good defense. They said it was extremely quiet and very dark, with no moon to light up

the area. After some cold chow, they dug defensive foxholes around the perimeter. The guards set up their lines of crossfire (in case of an attack) and took their posts to watch and listen for VC. The company had several new boots, and this was their first time in combat. It's the responsibility of the sergeant in charge to check all the guard positions throughout the night to make sure the men are awake and alert. Saleaumua was approaching one of the guard positions when the VC started their ground attack. The Samoan never had a chance; he was hit and died instantly. The medic tried but could not save him, and the chopper came in and removed his body from the CP.

I just can't believe it. One minute he was with us, and the next he was gone! Saleaumua was a good guy and good sergeant, and we are really going to miss him. After hearing the story, I couldn't help thinking it could have been me. I am so torn and conflicted over my feelings—of relief that because I wasn't selected for the mission I am alive, and my guilt that because Saleaumua was selected, he is the one who was killed. Is survival just the luck of the draw?

Please say a prayer for him and his family, and for me. And try not to worry.

I'll write again soon.

Love, George

I recently discovered more information about Saleaumua. The military casualty listing and timelines for our battalion reported that he was a Samoan American inducted in Hawaii; possibly his parents were Samoan, and they had moved to Hawaii.

Dear Mom and Dad, 2/20/67

Yesterday I volunteered for a mail run to Da Nang, which is also a chance for a little R & R. I was driving our new Ford jeep with two other Marines riding shotgun. On our way, we stopped in a village bar. The popular beer is Tiger 33, which someone said is a mix of beer and formaldehyde. But it tastes pretty good, and I figure maybe it would preserve me longer—ha-ha. We were enjoying a few and attempting conversation with two young Vietnamese women from the village. With broken English and hand gestures, we gathered that they were going to a Buddhist shrine in a nearby cave and were inviting us to come along. Trusting the locals can be risky since some civilians actively help the Viet Cong guerillas, and soldiers have paid a high price for it. But I was interested in seeing the shrine and went along out of curiosity. Trying to be safe, we chose to watch from a distance as they performed their worship before a gold Buddha statue surrounded by incense sticks and some trinkets. As they kneeled and said their prayers, it made me think back to our church and how we pray as Christians. Though our beliefs are different, we still have things in common, and our individual faiths are still important to us.

After they finished their prayers, we walked back to the hamlet and talked with them for a little while. We learned that they were students attending school in Da Nang and their parents were farmers. We also learned a little about their religious beliefs, which I had to write down to remember. It was a good experience, and for a few hours we were able to relax and forget that we were in a battle zone where traps and ambushes were as likely as the rain. We kept alert the whole time, with one eye open for trouble and the reassurance of my .45 at my side.

It was time to leave, so we said good-bye and headed back to the war knowing that while we could have been attacked by the VC at any time, we were honored to be invited to spend time with these girls, hear about their life, and observe their culture. I really hope they will be okay.

Won't be long now,
Love, George

While writing this chapter, I researched the Buddhist Ten Truths and have referenced their meaning:

Buddhist morality is codified in the form of 10 precepts which require abstention from: (1) taking life; (2) taking what is not given; (3) committing sexual misconduct (interpreted as anything less than chastity for the monk and as sexual conduct contrary to proper social norms, such as adultery, for the layman); (4) engaging in false speech; (5) using intoxicants; (6) eating after midday; (7) participating in worldly amusements; (8) adorning the body with ornaments and using perfume; (9) sleeping on high and luxurious beds; and (10) accepting gold and silver.[1]

Looks like I flunked Buddhism 101 at too much pleasure and intoxication. So far I have been able to avoid taking life unless you count the baby rats, and I sincerely hope that will not happen.

Dear Mom and Dad, 2/25/67
Last week I was asked by our gunnery sergeant to drive one of our lieutenants and another soldier to a nearby outpost that was regularly attacked by VC. The lieutenant said to drive and he would give the directions. It was raining as usual, and the road was in bad shape. Muddy potholes and raging streams crossing the road had slowed us down, and the weather and road conditions were good for Charlie to ambush us, so we were at the ready and expecting something to happen. As we came down a road, I noticed that a stream from a river had washed out a right curve, and we were going way too fast to make it. Seemed like a perfect VC ambush. I told everyone to get down and took the curve and stream at full speed. Fortunately we had the new jeep, and it handled extremely well. All of a sudden the jeep slid left, then right, and headed straight for the river. At the last moment, the front right wheel caught a rut in the road, and we made it around the curve. I thought the lieutenant was going to shoot me, but he just gestured to keep moving. This entire incident reminded me of an old Keystone Cops movie. Another close call—#10 if we're counting. When we arrived at the outpost, the lieutenant looked at me, and I'm sure he wanted to let me have it, but he just stared at me and said, "When we go back, we will take another road, Sergeant."

I was talking to Mike, one of the radio operators at the outpost, and he mentioned that they get nightly attacks by Charlie trying to find weak areas in their perimeter of defense. "Our outpost would send out a squad at night, and they would set up ambushes for Charlie. It could be uneventful, or all hell could break loose." He was pretty calm describing all this considering their constant state of alert. Personally, I couldn't wait to Get the Hell Out of There! The lieutenant gave us the sign to saddle up, as it was getting late and not safe to travel at night. The rain let up, and the roads were in better shape. I kept the vehicle under control this time, and we returned to our hooch safe and sound. Don't worry, Dad. Most of the time we are walking, not driving.

That's it for now.
Love, George

Dear Mom and Dad, 3/1/67

Better sit down for this one. Last night, after a 6-hour radio shift in the CP, I went to bed and crashed, only to be awakened by the sound of automatic rifle fire. Men were yelling something as I jumped out of bed. This wasn't a dream! Someone shouted that we were being hit by a sapper team (NVA demolition commandos). I grabbed my .45, boots, flak jacket, and helmet. (I am glad no one took a picture of me in my helmet and skivvies, fully armed and ready.) As I ran outside, I heard M14s and AK47s popping all around the camp. It was very dark and very confusing not knowing the locations of the sappers or who to shoot at. I crouched down, and before I could make out what was happening, it was over, lasting only about 5–10 minutes. The sergeant of the guards gave the all clear, and I went back to my bed shaking, adrenaline pumping hard. It took some time for me to get back to sleep, but eventually I dozed off.

We know about sapper attacks, but this was a first for us. They had set up a surprise attack on one side of our perimeter as bait to draw our attention away from the other side so the others could break through. I'm not sure what averted their plan, but nothing was blown up, and thankfully we had no casualties. Could be that our guards were very alert that night. In combat you need to sleep with one eye open. We were lucky this time, but I haven't gotten a full night's sleep since. Close call #11.
Love, George

I did a little research about sappers and found the following information and history. Sappers are well-trained special NVA soldiers (demolition commandos) who can wreak havoc and death with satchel charges (explosives in a bag that are easily carried and thrown), RPGs (rocket-propelled grenades), grenades, and automatic rifle fire. They are trained in demolitions and penetration techniques. Sappers can penetrate undetected through the outer defenses and launch an attack from inside the perimeter of defense. They gather intel by day and plan the most effective way to attack by night. Finding weak areas of perimeter defense and knowing what buildings to attack give them a distinct advantage. Attacking from within the perimeter creates confusion, especially when the sentries are being cautious not to fire at friendlies or our guys. The attacks rarely last longer than a few minutes, and the sappers exit by their preplanned route. The origin of the sappers goes back to the Indochina Wars.

> Dear Mom and Dad, 3/5/67
>
> I was asked to help out with one of our Combined Action Companies (CACs). They were short a radio operator and needed me to stand in for a few days until the replacement came in. The CAC unit is made up of a rifle squad and a corpsman that live in a Vietnamese rural hamlet. The idea is to live with the Vietnamese, set up a perimeter of defense, and work with the ARVIN to stop the VC from intimidating villagers. It's also a great intel source. I was transported there on a back road by a jeep. As we approached, I could see children running around playing, laundry being hung, and men fishing in the nearby river, with the smell of smoke wafting from the hamlet's cooking fires. The houses were made of the typical bamboo construction, centered around the campfires. I noticed water buffalo off to one side and some chickens and dogs running loose. Sort of reminds me of the nearby farms at home with cows instead of water buffalo, ha-ha. The hamlet elders came up to meet me and took me to the hut the CAC unit was using. The Marines were glad to see me, and over beers we talked about the mission of CAC and not trusting the ARVIN. Both the Marines and ARVIN had only had a few encounters with the VC so far and were able to fend them off.
>
> The first night was rough—I got no sleep, and I kept imagining VC killing or capturing us. The next day I met with several families, and relying on the ARVIN to help me with the language, I began to learn their names. The hamlet was constructed next to a river, so they had fresh fish and vegetables, which beats the hell out of the C-rats we get! It's very odd to know the war is all around you, but for the moment, time seemed to have stopped in this little hamlet. But we can never let down our guard, knowing Charlie may appear again.
>
> We were helping them with medical care and teaching personal hygiene and sanitation, and each day brought us a little closer with the Vietnamese people and an appreciation for their way of life. I made friends with two young boys. Every day they would stop by my hut and call my name (Sergeant George) to come out and fish, and they taught me a few things I didn't know. I don't remember what kind of fish we were catching, but when cooked with local herbs, it was outstanding. It was nice to have real food again, and though I started sleeping a little better, I never really got a full night's sleep.
>
> Before I knew it, 4 days had passed, and the replacement radio operator arrived to relieve me. I was sorry to leave and wish I could have stayed and helped protect them, but I said good-bye to my two little friends and the elders, got on the jeep, and left for Camp Phu Bai. This was one experience I will be happy to remember. It's a reminder that though people all over the world may have different cultures and beliefs, in the most important ways we are also alike—no better and no worse, just trying to live our lives and take care of our families and help where we can. Can't wait to get home and see everyone.
>
> Have to go for now.
> Love, George

During my research, I found that the concept of CAC can be traced back to conflicts in Haiti, Nicaragua, and the Dominican Republic. The Marine Corps initiated CAC in Vietnam during 1965 near Phu Bai. The redefined CAC missions were to have a Marine rifle squad and a Navy medic and to team up with a platoon of ARVIN or RF (Regional Forces). The team's mission was to help the ARVIN guard, protect, and do nightly S & D, providing security, civil actions, roads, schools, wells, and medical care for the villagers. I remember calling the teams CAC units but later found out they changed the name to Combined Action Program (CAP) due to a Vietnamese issue with the acronym "CAC" (their word for the male generative organ).

The CAP program helped the Marines to understand the Vietnamese culture as well as to develop trust, resulting in friendships and good intel. The program also kept the VC out of the village and stopped them from drafting the young and taking valuable food supplies from the villagers.

Most of the men assigned to the CAP units were specially trained in counterinsurgency, civil actions, and rural politics in the CAP school in Da Nang. Like most training, the real training starts when you are in the field under actual conditions. By 1969 the program grew to 19 companies, 102 platoons, and 4 groups. The CAP units operated in Nam from 1965–1971. The program proved to be a highly effective counterinsurgency arm for the Marine Corps.[2]

Dear Mom and Dad,   *3/10/67*
Just returned from a joint mission with the Vietnamese army and a squad of our men. Our commander was asked to send a rifle team to support an ARVIN company which was acting on intel that VC were active in an area north of Phu Bai. We left early in the morning by foot and kept close to the shore of a small river. As a short-timer, I admit to being nervous. Actually that is an understatement, but I had to keep my wits about me. Fortunately, the men in the rifle squad had been in country for 6–8 months, and I was counting on their experience to get us back safe and sound. In a few hours we hooked up with the ARVIN and continued north. We followed the river to a heavily wooded area with rice-paddy fields as far as you could see.

It was getting late and time to dig in, so we stopped at an open area that was close to the river, dug foxholes and set up a perimeter defense, chowed down on the C-rats, and got some rest. I was lucky—my dinner in a can was spaghetti and meatballs, one of the most acceptable meals.

The lieutenant and I were burrowing in, trying to get comfortable in our shallow foxhole and attempting to sleep with one eye open. The night was like tar, with no moonshine or stars, and I had just begun to drift off when suddenly the entire camp was ablaze with exploding satchel charges (explosive demolition bags—basically very large grenades) and blasts of gunfire. I could briefly see people through the flashes of light, and then they were lost in the darkness. It became a free-for-all, with men shouting, running, and firing their weapons. The ARVIN captain somehow made his way to our foxhole to let the lieutenant know that we were being attacked by VC and that some of the ARVIN were VC. This was bad. We could not tell who to shoot at, and it was getting more intense. The captain said the VC were overrunning our position and that we needed artillery support.

The lieutenant tore my radio handset from me and called in three rounds of 155 howitzers on our own CP coordinates. He told everyone to get down and grab their asses. He wasn't kidding! I have never been on the receiving end of a 155 or any other artillery. The incoming rounds were like a freight train coming down the track. It got louder and louder until it hit, then the entire ground rose about a foot and lowered back down with us in it, and I thought we were going to die. There was some hand-to-hand combat going on, but by the time the rounds from the 155 stopped, the battle was over, and except for the flicker of flashlights it was just as dark again. I could feel my heart pumping like I just ran a 440 and my hands were shaking, but I was alive.

The ARVIN had defeated the VC, but they had many casualties. Our campsite was pockmarked with craters, and I stared through the haze of smoke, astonished that anyone had survived. Our patrol was lucky, only a few scratches and some loss of hearing. Early morning, we called in a medevac for the ARVIN soldiers who were wounded, and I threw a smoke canister out so the chopper could locate us. As the Huey landed, I carried one of the wounded ARVIN soldiers to the side door and carefully placed him inside. Another ARVIN tapped me on my shoulder as he laid the wounded man's shoe inside the chopper. I did a double take and stared in amazement as I realized that his foot was still in the shoe. The man did not scream or even cry out. He just looked up and thanked me, and I thought, Dear God, through unimaginable pain, horror, and fear, there is still such bravery.

At daybreak, we left the camp and started to work our way back to Phu Bai, navigating through several fields of rice paddies. We figured the VC had laid mines in the fields, so every step was cautiously taken, knowing it could be our last. I thought for sure that my time was coming. Just one more step, then another and another. . . . Finally we got out of the fields to the dirt road and made our way back to camp. There are no words for how glad I was to set foot in that mangy camp. I could have kissed that muddy ground and smelly old tent! We were starved and glad to get some hot chow and, oh yeah, more than a few beers!!

That was close call #12, but I made it back safe again! Won't be long now.
Love, George

Dear Mom and Dad,   *3/15/67*
Great news. The top sergeant told me that I had transfer orders to report to Da Nang to work in the Fire Direction Center (FDC). I said good-bye to my friends and grabbed the first available truck out. Looking back as Phu Bai disappeared in the dust, I thought about Paul and Operations Prairie and Hastings. Those events were indelibly etched in my mind and heart, and I will carry it and relive it for the rest of my life.

We arrived late afternoon at an artillery battery a few miles north of Da Nang. I reported in to the first sergeant, and he assigned me to a hooch near the mess hall. What luck—walking distance for chow and the latrine! I wasted no time getting a hot shower and making myself at home. One of the guys had hired a local mama-san to keep the hooch clean and do our laundry. She was a young woman, gentle and quiet and always smiling. Everyone appreciated the work she did to keep our uniforms clean and pressed, and we tipped her well. I gave her my fatigues and crashed on my freshly made cot.

They gave me a day to get acquainted and then assigned me the evening radio shift. The duty is pretty good. Our CP was running all-day and all-night support for U.S. and ARVIN troops. I just had to take the radio shifts and wait for a call to run a fire mission for any troops in trouble. One afternoon while on duty, I was asked to help a wounded Vietnamese official get on a Huey. I went to a dirt pad near the airfield and found a gray-haired Vietnamese man in traditional dress waiting for me. I greeted him with a salute, and he replied, "Hello, Sergeant," in surprisingly good English. I asked where he was from, and he said he was an official for some township in Da Nang. While waiting for his ride, we had a chance to talk for a few minutes. I told him that I was a short-timer and would soon be leaving Vietnam and then home to Pennsylvania. He shared his dream of coming to the U.S. someday with his family. Like many people we've met here, he dreamed of living in America where he and his family could live in peace, free from the fear of war.

I heard the sound of the chopper and threw out the green smoke, which indicates a secure landing spot. We stood there in the rising dust waiting for the chopper to touch down. The rotors slowed, and I ducked down and carried the man to the open door. As they took off, he waved, thanked me for my help, and yelled, "See you in America!" Once again, I was amazed at the gratitude and humility of the Vietnamese people, and I was filled with a sense of relief that in the midst of the killing there is still kindness and shared hope for all of us.

I only have 3 to 4 more weeks left until I have my travel papers to rotate back to the States. Believe me, I'm trying my damnedest to get there alive. When I'm not working at the FDC, I stay in my hooch most of the time. I've made it this far through this God-forsaken war, and I don't want to press my luck! I will call you when I get stateside. I fly into Los Angeles and then directly to Philadelphia, and I'll let you know when I will arrive. Please do not have a big reception for me; just friends and family would be nice. My mind is full of plans for my future, and I've definitely made the decision to apply for art school when I return. I can use the GI Bill to help pay for it. Not sure what I want to do with the rest of my life, but getting back in school would be a good start. I am going to use some of my combat pay to get a sports car, any color but green. That should make my friends envious. Mom, I cannot wait to have one of your outstanding meat-and-potatoes dinners. Dad, I will even help cut that grass, ha-ha. Don't forget to warn the local girls I am coming home soon.

Time for chow. See you real soon.
Love, George

The day finally came to leave Vietnam, and I received my orders to return to Camp Lejeune, North Carolina. I wasted no time in packing, saying goodbye, and crossing off the last day of my short-time calendar. I'm pretty sure I had a stupid grin on my face, and it felt like I was floating on air. I hitched a jeep ride to Da Nang where I would board a C-130 troop transport plane for Kadena, Okinawa, with the rest of the short-timers, checked in, and waited. We do a lot of waiting in the military, but this was the good kind of waiting. After a few hours, they called us to board. Walking to the plane, my heart was pumping, and I found myself still looking around for snipers and sappers, even knowing that the airport was relatively safe from attacks. I couldn't completely relax as my mind wandered to things that might go wrong. What if a VC rocket takes out the plane, or what if the plane has engine failure?

We headed back to Okinawa so we could pick up our duffle bags containing our uniforms and civilian clothes left behind when we first arrived. As the plane gained altitude, I gazed out the small window at the landscape I had come to know so well during those ten months. Staring at the blue sky and scattered puffs of clouds, it was almost impossible to imagine the horror below, and I tried to remove the images of new troops coming in who would continue the effort and face the daily terror of life and death that I was, thankfully, leaving behind.

We finally landed in Kadena, located our gear, and waited to board a commercial airline headed back to the States. Now back in Okinawa, my mind was racing with so many thoughts, including Suzuki and the time we had together. But there had been no time to find her nor a phone number to call. I was daydreaming of her gentle touch and long, black flowing hair when one of the guys sitting next to me bumped my arm and said we were boarding. I doubted whether I would ever get back to Okinawa again and kept thinking, when I get on this plane, she will just be a beautiful memory. Once inside and seated, I loosened up a little as I noticed the clean, fresh smell of the interior and the lack of diesel fumes. I realized how tense I was when an attractive stewardess leaned over and asked if I wanted some refreshments. With appreciation, I ordered two beers. I have to admit the brew helped to calm my nerves and turn my thoughts to pleasanter things, and before I knew it we were in the air.

The plane was loaded with both civilians and military personnel. It was ironic that I was flying the friendly skies in comfort, with offers of cocktails, while back in Vietnam—this beautiful place of peaceful people—the earth was being devastated, with farmlands and rice paddies providing the stage for killing fields. For the replacements, it was the beginning of their nightmare. For me, it was the end. I was finally returning home, and I couldn't wait for my life to begin again.

NO PLACE LIKE HOME   14

The flight attendant's voice broke the silence announcing our descent. "Please make sure your seat backs and trays are in the upright position. Be sure your seat belt is securely fastened, and remain seated until the captain turns off the Fasten Seat Belt sign." The captain announced that we had arrived. "Ladies and Gentlemen, welcome to Los Angeles International Airport. On behalf of United Airlines and the entire crew, I'd like to thank you for joining us on this flight, and we look forward to seeing you on board again in the near future. Also, we'd like to welcome home our soldiers and thank you for your service."

I could see the smog around the city as we made a smooth landing on the runway. After thirteen months away in Japan and Vietnam. I was almost home and anxiously waited as we taxied to the gate. The minute my feet touched American soil, I was overcome with emotion, and my relief was palpable. This time, instead of intense heat and the overpowering smell of diesel fuel assailing my nostrils, I stepped into fresh air, the smell of flowers, and the hubbub of normal, everyday life. The airport was filled with brightly colored posters with images of flowers and rainbows sending inviting messages of travel to faraway places in the sun and fun—none of which were in Vietnam.

The first real impact was the visible difference in the appearance of the people. The clothing style, which I came to know as hippie dress, was surprising. Both boys and girls had long hair past their shoulders and wore sandals or high boots. There were protestors parading with bold signs of "Make Love, Not War," and vets wearing jeans and T-shirts with jungle jackets, carrying peace signs. In spite of the protestors, the war was still very far away, and everyone was going about their business. As I made my way through the airport, it occurred to me that while we were fighting and dying for some vague cause on the other side of the world, I wasn't convinced the average person understood what was really going on in Vietnam and most probably didn't really care about the daily struggle of the Vietnamese people for survival. Except for the families who had lost a son or daughter to this obscure war and for whom life had changed indelibly, it was just another day, and we were just guys walking around in fatigues.

Now stateside, it appeared to me that most Americans seemed indifferent to the theft of freedom, dignity, and joy of the Vietnamese people, for whom they had no real understanding. But little did I realize the magnitude or the importance of the war protest that was unfolding while I was in Vietnam. On April 4, 1967, the day before I arrived back in the States, Dr. Martin Luther King Jr., one of our greatest spiritual leaders, was on the march and spoke at the Riverside Church in New York City, giving a speech that was true to the heart and the people of Vietnam. I had only heard about Reverend King from some of the guys that were arriving in Nam in early 1967. In later years, I read his speech and could not believe how he could see through the politics and grasp the reality of the Vietnamese plight.

Dr. King was asking our government to stop the Vietnam War and end the carnage and suffering of both the American people and the Vietnamese people. So little is gained, and so much is lost. Our government started this war, and they have the power to end it. To read the entire speech, please go to www.commondreams.org ("Beyond Vietnam").[1]

A week later, on April 15, 1967, there was a massive antiwar protest and draft-card burning in New York and Los Angeles. I remember being confused about the war and the antiwar movement. I think by then most of the country was asking the same question—what are our sons and daughters dying for? I just kept hanging on to the belief that the Vietnamese people had the right to be free as we all do, and freedom very often comes at a high price.

The flight to Philadelphia airport arrived early afternoon, and as I walked through the terminal exit gate, my heart was pounding with excitement and the anticipation of being home. Home, the place we all sat talking about in our hooch. Home, where life would be ours again, where we would be with loved ones and could make plans for our futures.

As excited as I was to see everyone, I hadn't thought about the actual reunion. Suddenly surrounded by my entire family and being showered with hugs and happy tears, the realization hit me of how proud they were of my service and how filled with relief for my safe return. The last leg of my journey was the hour drive to our suburban Bucks County home where I'd lived since early childhood, and I began to relax into the pleasure of recognizing familiar places on the way. When we finally arrived at home and I realized nothing had changed, I was comforted by the familiarity. My room was exactly as it was when I left four years ago—the same blanket with images of horses on my twin bed, the same lumpy mattress, and my old black-and-white TV that had entertained me and my friends for countless, carefree hours. The closet still had my clothes from high school, and the bookcase and walls displayed familiar childhood collections. With complete contentment I hadn't known for a long time, I lay down in my bed, closed my eyes, and surrendered to a sleep I forgot existed.

The next day, Mom and Dad announced that they had planned a homecoming party for me over the weekend. Until then I had a few days to rest and re-acclimate. I borrowed Dad's car and drove to my friend's house for a surprise visit and realized again how much I'd missed home and everyone. Later I drove to our local hangout, a greasy spoon, hoping to see familiar faces and meet up with old friends. To my relief, not that much had changed. It was still the local hangout, and I did see some of the hoped-for familiar faces. With happy greetings, back-slaps, and an invitation to join some guys in their booth, I settled down in that familiar setting and ordered my favorite drink and food—cherry Coke, fries, and a hamburger—and dove into my meal as though I hadn't eaten during those four years of service. Hanging out again almost made me feel like it never happened, like it was just a long, horrible nightmare—almost. Eager to hear news of all I had missed, I wasn't prepared for all the questions about Nam, especially whether I had killed anyone, which I managed to avoid answering. I didn't want to talk about what happened there, and I knew they could never understand anyway. As I sat in that restaurant booth trying to enjoy the casual conversation and gossip, I had to fight off the memories and images of Vietnam that attempted to surface. I just wanted to leave the horror behind, move forward, and get on with life. Over and over I silently thanked God that I made it back alive and unharmed, but I would come to know that as much as I concentrated on the now, the war experiences would always be with me, like a specter that haunted my thoughts. I had no idea what to do with the feelings, and so pushed I them deeper into the back of my mind, hoping to be free. But every so often I would find myself back in the jungle, or at night, waking from a deep sleep, yelling out Paul's name. To this day, I am still haunted with visions of Paul, alone, calling for help, and the guilt that I am alive while so many lives were lost in one insane moment when they were at the wrong place at the wrong time.

Our little house was bursting with friends, neighbors, and our minister who came to celebrate with our family. I could tell they were genuinely happy for my safe return and relieved for the end to my parents' worries. This type of happy scene would play out across America for the lucky ones who, after collectively holding their breath those long months, finally exhaled with relief and rejoiced together for their child's return to the fold. But for us, the soldiers, it would take some time to transition to civilian life, time before we could stop pinching ourselves to be sure we were really awake. The warm reception of those caring people helped, and watching Mom and Dad, I could see the strain leave their faces as they could finally relax and rejoice at having our family together again. As people joked about my language when I referred to the head or latrine, mess hall, etc., I also realized that I needed to readjust to using civilian language. The military has its own, and Marines have a very special and unique vocabulary that I definitely had to leave behind.

Dad broke the news to me that my car had died, but fortunately I'd sent home over $3,000 combat pay. We figured that would pay for the sports car I had been thinking about in Nam, and maybe with some money left over. The next day I drove to a large car dealership in the neighboring town of Bristol. They had over five acres of cars, new and used. After several hours of looking, I found a 1964 Red Jaguar XKE convertible with low mileage. I test-drove it in the dealer's test lot and fell in love. For $2,400 I drove my dream car off the lot, and as Dad said, I had a little cash left over. This car performed incredibly and had a top end of 140 miles per hour. The engine was a straight six with trip Webbers. The word got out to the guys, and as I had with my first car, I became instantly popular. Everyone wanted to see it and go for a ride.

After a great week of R & R, I gathered my things, filled my duffel bag, and hugged my parents before leaving to report back to Camp Lejeune to finish my enlistment. Driving the XKE made the eight-hour trip faster and, with the top down, all the more enjoyable. Arriving at the base in my new ride created lots of attention, and, no surprise, I made more new friends. I was assigned to a communications company as radio operator. We had trucks that were specially designed for field communications with high-power transmitters. Because I was a senior sergeant, I had my own room in the barracks. I put my things away and hung up another short-time calendar on the wall, this one so different from the one in Nam where I had counted the days to home that I hoped to make it alive.

Almost every weekend I would get the XKE and drive the shorelines and pristine beaches of North and South Carolina. Rooms were not too expensive, so I could stay for the weekend and get in my beach time. I remember one weekend I overslept at a hotel and woke up an hour before the morning formation at Lejeune. Our company formation is 6:30 a.m. to verify that everyone is present. If anyone is missing, the Corps could charge them as unauthorized absence (UA)—which is an offense with some brig time. I ran out to the hotel parking lot, jumped in the XKE, and took off like a bat out of hell. I had to be on base in one hour, and I was 1.5 hours away. Fortunately the roads in North Carolina were straight, so I took the XKE up to 120 mph while looking for police. The car started to vibrate at 100, but when it hit 110 the nose just settled down and the car became a bullet. I pulled into the base with ten minutes to spare, parked the car, and ran as fast as I could to join the formation. I had fallen asleep in my uniform, so I was able to slip into the rear ranks, and as they called my name, I yelled, "Yo!"

After three more months I finished out my regular enlistment, and in August 1967 I received my honorable discharge papers. I wasted no time driving home, back to my family, friends, and future. During my high school days, the art teacher said I had some talent, so I applied to the Hussian School of Art in Philadelphia hoping she was right. While attending high school, I had taken some drafting classes that prepared me for work with my father's company as an electrical draftsman. After completing four years in the military, ten months of it spent in the special hell of war, my civilian life was launched!

LIFE GOES ON   15

It's hard to believe that close to forty years have passed since that rainy evening at the office in 1985. Driving home from work that night, I realized that I wanted to record my memories to share my piece of history, and the idea of a book began to take shape as short stories in the form of letters never sent home. In 2012, I retired and began devoting more time to research, with no real idea of how big an undertaking it would be to verify information about operations and missions, research weaponry, and construct a timeline of events for accurate dates. Writing the letters released the floodgates of forgotten details and buried emotions, and many times I have wondered if I'm up to the task to which I've committed myself.

One of the most critical items for the book was to find where my friend Paul was buried and if he had any family still living. I also needed to find Bill Wright (mentioned in chapter 11, "Operation Prairie"). In 2014, my nephew Kim Tyson offered his help and that of some friends to locate Bill, whom they discovered living in New York, and it was the breakthrough I had hoped for. I was a bit apprehensive about making the call, not knowing whether he would care to hear from me or talk about the past. Finally I mustered the nerve and was honestly surprised by my emotions at the sound of his voice. As I quickly explained who I was and the reason for my call, I felt myself tear up.

We talked on two occasions, each for several hours, and he shared with me the difficult decisions and extreme measures he took to keep his men alive and what happened to Paul in Operation Prairie. As he also relayed information about other operations, his voice became loud and angry, and I was torn between continuing or ending the conversation, knowing he was on an emotional roller-coaster of memories. I decided to switch gears, and we spoke a while longer, sharing news about our current lives and families, then agreeing to connect again in the future.

After the war, Bill joined the Brooklyn, New York, Police Department and served honorably until he retired. He said he always wanted to write a book about his military experiences, so in a small way Bill's story has found a way into mine. I want to thank him for his willingness to share that part of his life, for his heroism, and for his devoted service throughout his life.

My nephew's friends also found Paul's family information and burial location where he rests in Roanoke, Virginia, near the home of his sister Theresa. His mother, father, and brother have passed away, and she is his only remaining relative. Through a letter of introduction sent by the commander of my VFW (Post 845), I was able to contact Theresa, and almost immediately I received an email from her saying she would be honored to hear from me and talk about Paul. Finally, after the long years of carrying my promise to him, it was becoming a reality. The phone was beckoning me, and with trepidation, I started to dial the number several times before committing to the task, waiting in anticipation for the voice to welcome me and ease my years of anxiety. The voice that answered had a warm southern accent that reminded me of Paul, and again I felt tears forming as I introduced myself to her.

During that first call, I told Theresa how much I had mourned Paul and admitted my guilt for not being able to save him or contact his family sooner. I recounted the entire story of Operation Prairie and what Bill and I tried to do to save Paul. She was gracious and forgiving and told me she was grateful that so many men tried their best to reach Paul under impossible conditions. We talked at length, sharing stories about our families and lives, agreeing to correspond by email in the future before saying good-bye. After years of imagining that conversation, I felt drained of all emotion and sat staring into space with no cohesive thoughts. But it was accomplished, and I was exhausted and in need of dreamless sleep. Theresa wrote a few days later and said, on behalf of her family, that they understood and forgave me. Seeing those words eased the guilt I had carried for so long, and it was as if Paul had reached through the past to say, "It's okay, George. I know you and Bill did your best." Shortly after I contacted Theresa, my wife Anita and I began to plan a trip to Virginia.

On Memorial Day weekend in 2014, we traveled to Roanoke to meet Theresa, her husband Robert, and their two young granddaughters, Ieslen and Rain. That Sunday we met for the first time at their family church and worshipped together. Ieslen, the youngest granddaughter, gave me a picture she had drawn of her great-uncle Paul in Vietnam. I sensed Paul's presence as though watching our meeting through my eyes. After worship, we gathered at a local restaurant for lunch and spent some time getting to know each other. Theresa's granddaughters, who are the same ages as ours, shared their interests and activities, and we easily connected. Our shared sorrow over losing Paul bonded us as friends. At times it seemed dreamlike, as though I was watching from a distance, and I kept pulling myself back to the present, later telling my wife that it was hard to believe we were finally here together.

Before leaving the restaurant, they agreed to meet at our hotel by the swimming pool to continue our talk about Paul and their family and to discuss my progress on the book. The girls frolicked in the water, their young, laughing voices fading into the background as Theresa began her story, revealing all that had happened here at home while Paul and I were on the other side of the world. When Paul died, she was only ten, but she remembered that her mom, Margaret, and her dad, Rodney, received a letter from Paul telling them about being wounded in the arm by enemy fire. The letter arrived before the Marines showed up to inform them of his injury. For the family, the important thing had been that Paul was still sending letters home, which meant he was okay. But then something changed. Below is Theresa's memory of those tragic days before and following the news of Paul's death, as seen through the eyes of a ten-year-old and told forty-plus years later.

Theresa remembered that three or four weeks had passed, when on the morning of August 27, 1966, their lives were changed forever. Theresa said,

> You hear of premonitions . . . well, days before we received word of Paul being killed, we did things that we normally wouldn't do. My mom thoroughly cleaned our house. You have to understand my mom was not a perfect housekeeper. On any given day there would be 4–5 pairs of shoes lined up on the floor, a day's worth of newspapers lying on the couch, and a sink full of dirty dishes. Things weren't dirty, just not tidy, so to speak, but during those days. all these things now had to be cleared away. Maybe it had something to do with us being notified just a month earlier by the USMC that my brother had been injured in the arm by enemy fire.
>
> My mother received Paul's letter before the Marines came to tell us. Maybe this was a way of preparing us for what was to come. Dad was a long-haul truck driver and only home one day a week, so mowing the lawn fell on mom's to-do list. My brother Jack, who rarely helped around the house, had just gotten out of the Army. He was bored and had reenlisted, so he had other things on his mind, but suddenly to everyone's surprise, he mowed the lawn. We didn't have air-conditioning in our house—just open windows with box fans, and I generally slept in just my underwear, but this night I had put on my clown pj's. In that heat I don't know why I would have done that.
>
> On Saturday morning, August 27, around 9 a.m., I got up, looked out the front window, and saw a USMC captain and our parish priest walking toward our door. I called for my mom, who grabbed her housecoat and answered the door. When she saw our priest, she knew my brother had been killed and

began to cry, as did I. I don't remember where my brother Jack was, but he was not home. My dad was out of town, and we had no way to contact him. All I remember my mom asking was, "Are you bringing him home?" Capt. Renner said, "Yes, we are making arrangements now." They stayed a while, prayed with us, and then left. My mom called where my dad worked, and all they knew was that he was due in that afternoon, so my mom proceeded to make phone calls. My dad's friends were on the lookout for him and discovered he had stopped off at the local tavern on his way home to have a beer with some of his fellow drivers. Seeing his close friend walk in, my dad knew something wasn't right and immediately said, "He's gone, isn't he?" Somehow he just knew. All I remember doing during that time was sitting in the yard with my dog, crying as never before.

It seemed like an eternity before we finally got word that Paul's body would be arriving early in September by train with a personal escort. Knowing finally allowed arrangements to begin. Word traveled fast, and the steady stream of friends, family, food, cards, notes, flowers, etc. began to flow in. So many people came to our house that we had to rent chairs, and my parents also decided to rent an air conditioner for the house to keep everyone comfortable. We also had family traveling in from Pennsylvania. I remember when Paul finally arrived home, his escort came to our house. Sgt. Mike Garcia was there to be with us. He was a kind young man who stayed with us from morning to early evening and until after the funeral service, just being supportive and helping out however he could. Neighbors would come in and mop floors, run the vacuum, clean whatever was needed, and brought food, oh so much food.

Paul was a very likable guy. He had many friends from school and football and from the places he worked before joining the Marines. At the visitation that lasted two days, it seemed all of Roanoke stopped by for its fallen Marine. Paul had been shot in the head, so we had a closed casket service on the advice of Sgt. Garcia. My dad always thought it was a mistaken identity and hoped Paul would someday come home, but my mother told the funeral home if she could just see his one hand and arm, she would know because he had a scar. She had them look, and they confirmed that it was indeed my brother.

Paul's girlfriend was a nurse from North Carolina. They wanted to marry, but he told her to wait until he came home because he did not want to leave her a widow. We had never met her but had her name and contact information, and my parents called to tell her of Paul's death. My dad was in a local restaurant when a woman and young lady who stopped for breakfast bought a local newspaper and saw that the paper had Paul's picture and story. As the young lady was paying her bill, she asked if they knew Paul. My dad heard her and answered, "Yes, that is my son." Discovering she was Paul's girlfriend and was there for the funeral, they followed dad home where they met everyone. I remember her as a very sweet person.

Paul was given a full military ceremony. Being Catholic, we also had a Mass of the Resurrection followed by the graveside service where I received the flag from his casket presented to me by Capt. Renner who had come to our house. I couldn't tell you what he said. I just remember gripping it tightly and not wanting to let it go. Sgt. Garcia kept telling me to let it go, just let it fall into the plastic cover, and I guess I finally did.

I remember to this day the last time I saw Paul alive. He was at the gate boarding the plane heading for California dressed in his winter uniform, standing straight, tall, and proud. We exchanged letters, none of which made sense to me then, but after reading them over time I know he is in heaven because he was in hell while in Vietnam. Paul would always end his letters to my parents, "Tell TM (Theresa Marie) to light a candle for me." Something I would do every Sunday at church.

Telling the story of how Theresa's family learned of Paul's death has been difficult for both of us, and I thank her for sharing what is so intensely painful and personal. Instead of Arlington, they choose to bury Paul at home in their local cemetery in Roanoke. According to Theresa, her parents never really recovered from the loss of their son.

We talked about Paul and his family for several hours, and Theresa told me that their brother Jack had been in Vietnam at the same time Paul was there, which is very surprising because the military generally would not assign siblings to a combat zone at the same time. This must have caused unimaginable stress for his parents and family. In later life, Jack was diagnosed with severe diabetes, heart problems, and Agent Orange symptoms. He died in March 2012. Their parents had passed away prior to that, so they were spared the pain of losing two sons. Theresa had to endure the loss of a second brother, but she stayed at Jack's side throughout his struggle to the end. Currently she is raising her two young granddaughters, in spite of health problems of her own. I salute her for having the courage to take on with love what few but a grandparent would consider without hesitation.

It was getting late, so we parted and agreed to meet at the cemetery Monday morning. Early on Memorial Day 2014, we met at Paul's grave where I had flowers delivered for our ceremony. Standing at attention in a full-dress blue uniform in front of my friend's marker, I was thinking, "Why Paul and not me?" I was trembling and on the verge of tears but pulled myself together to read the poem "Immortality," often used by the Veterans of Foreign Wars (VFW) as a Soldier's Prayer.

Immortality
Do not stand at my grave and weep,
I am not there, I do not sleep,
I am a thousand winds that blow,
I am the diamond that glints in the snow,
I am the sunlight on ripened grain,
I am the gentle autumn rain,
When you awaken in the morning hush,
I am the swift uplifting rush of quiet birds in circled flight,
I am the soft stars that shine at night,
Do not stand at my grave and cry,
I am not there. I did not die.[1]

After saying a few private words to Paul, I turned to Theresa and delivered Paul's message as promised so long ago. "Tell my parents it's okay. I am at peace. I love them, and I'm sorry I did not make it back." As Theresa and I hugged each other, I felt liberated from the burden I had carried all those years. I kept my promise to Paul made that night over beers, to visit his family if anything happened to him. My mission accomplished, I felt that Paul could finally rest.

When we were done, Ieslen, the youngest granddaughter, walked over and said she had something for me. Lifting her arm from behind her back, she properly presented me with Paul's ceremonial flag, given to his parents at his military funeral as a reminder that their loved one had not died in vain. Theresa told me the family wanted me to have the flag, and I stood there at a loss to express how deeply I was touched. There is no higher honor than receiving a warrior's flag, and I will keep and cherish it forever. Sharing final hugs and good-byes, we watched as Theresa and her family drove off. Then, silently saying good-bye to my friend, I gave a final salute to Paul, and we left. Theresa and I have continued our friendship and write often to share family news.

EPILOGUE

The idea of writing this book as a tribute to my friend Paul has become the story of a kid who became a man in a foreign land. Like so many, he witnessed explosions and slaughter, the shock and heartbreaking death of friends, and experienced extremes from seemingly endless boredom to instant, heart-pounding terror, and with it, the loss of innocence. But also the gift of friendship, and witness to the strength and character of men who became heroes.

There are still many days that I think about my friends Paul and Bill, along with so many others. Writing this memoir has helped me to make peace with the past, and I hope it has given the reader a glimpse of war through eyes of this grunt who journeyed with the true heroes. This story doesn't include the other heroes—actually heroines—the nurses who performed duties that stateside had only been performed by doctors, only to discover that their vast wartime knowledge was not of value. Working tirelessly to mend broken bodies, they also devoted long hours to reading letters, listening to stories, giving encouragement, and holding the hands of the dying. Yet these angels were often treated with the same disdain as the returning soldiers. Much has been written about women in combat and military nurses, for those interested.

Life experience helps to shape the people we become. Our futures were formed with each mission, each near miss, each dead body we encountered, and each bullet-torn soldier. Some of us make our way, while others continue to be haunted by the past. It is for all of them that as brothers and sisters we do what we can to help by raising funds and awareness for vets, placing flags on graves in remembrance, and walking alongside those who are still suffering physically or emotionally. And most of all, reminding our nation of their sacrifices and that real appreciation and support for the men and women who protect our nation has to be more tangible than waving a flag and, though always appreciated, only saying thank you for your service.

**May God bless our men and women in uniform
and their families, whose bravery and sacrifices
ensure that America may continue to be the land of the free.**

High School graduation photo of Paul Reed.

Photo of Paul in his dress green Marine Corps uniform.

Photo in front of the Marine Corps Iwo Jima War Memorial in Parris Island behind author, George Uhl, after graduation from boot camp.

Promotion of George to corporal (noncommissioned officer) just prior to receiving orders to ship out to Vietnam.

After field training for telephone wireman at Camp Lejeune, George received his MOS 2511 (wireman occupation).

Climbing thirty feet or more wearing spikes and a belt with rope for support, George pulls wire from the ground to string communication lines.

Navy transport docked before leaving for the Mediterranean.

Packed like sardines below deck, soldiers make the best of it playing pinochle and reading to pass the time while en route to the Mediterranean.

Stopping short of the edge of the deck, George captures friends pretending to jump ship.

Popular foot-shot view of the landing deck with helicopters, vehicles, and troops, captured as George relaxes on the deck of the transport ship leaving the states for the Mediterranean.

George by an H-37 Sikorsky Mojave transport helicopter wishing he could hop a ride to anywhere terra firma (except Nam).

George enjoying a cold mug of beer.

George with liberty buddy "Old Man" Frank Russo, who also hails from Philadelphia.

George and Russo on three-day liberty in Naples, Italy, looking for adventure.

Russo and his uncle who is a teacher in Naples. Together they all toured the area in his tiny Italian car that almost required a shoehorn to fit three tall men.

First stop in Naples was the zoo and a visit from this guy we called Sgt. Big Mouth.

We named the friendly two-hump camel Clyde.

Last day of liberty skiing the Italian Alps, standing out in front of the ski lodge.

Next stop on the cruise was Barcelona, Spain, for a mock landing exercise. George on the loading dock.

Slicker was no match for the rain in Spain that completely drenched George that day.

Chopping wood for some fireside warmth against the cold nights in tents.

Visit to Curaçao during Caribbean cruise after brief return to Camp Lejeune.

Main commerce street in Curaçao.

Back commercial street in Curaçao that merges with the fishing pier and ocean vessels.

Second Caribbean cruise to run fire mission on Snake Island, Puerto Rico.

Calling in an active forward artillery command and Fire Direction Center on the Snake Island firing range.

Waiting in front of quarters in the heat for beer rations that never showed up.

Unfortunately, some of the guys pulled MP (Military Police) duty in the small town in Snake Island during liberty.

Next stop, Da Nang. Marine sergeant welcomed us and promptly handed out flak jackets.

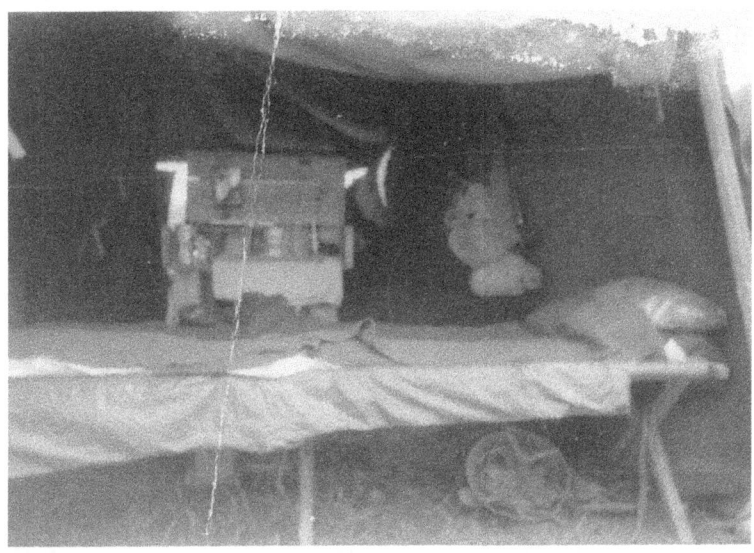

Accommodations in tents, known as hooches, were tight and hot.

Vietnamese open markets near camp in Phu Bai offer needs beyond military supplies.

Children at Vietnamese vendor booth in Phu Bai.

Merchants set up near next camp in Dong Ha.

Bird Dog spotter planes were made of bailing wire and duct tape and serve to spot the enemy for artillery.

Bathing in a basin.

Company sergeant having a beer in one of the vendor booths.

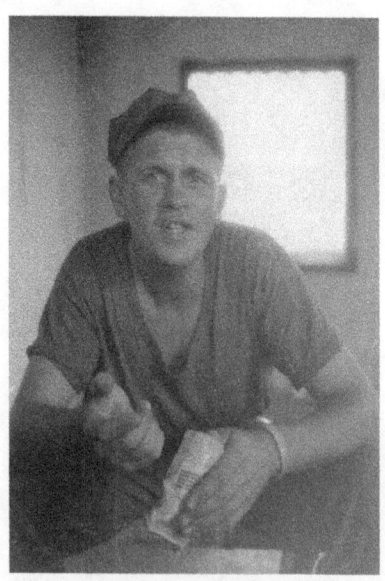

One of George's friends, "Charles was a little crazy, but he always had my back." Since passed away, he was one of the Corps' finest.

Another friend from the Mediterranean and Caribbean cruises, John was from New York, shown here at a vendor marketplace.

Paul's niece, Ieslen, gave this drawing to George paying tribute to Paul when they all met for the first time in Virginia.

Grave site with Ieslen and Rain, granddaughters of Paul's sister Theresa.

Ieslen presenting George with the military funeral flag from Paul's family at the Blue Ridge Cemetery in Roanoke, Virginia.

George in full uniform with Theresa at Paul's grave.

Paul's gravestone at the Roanoke cemetery.

Theresa's family at the cemetery.

George with wife Anita at Paul's gravestone presenting flowers and a prayer.

George holding Paul's flag by his grave.

ACKNOWLEDGMENTS

I would like to thank the people who offered help and encouragement over the years.

My wife, Anita, has been my most important support, relentlessly interviewing me to exhume long-forgotten memories of the child and boy I was, scrutinizing and examining sentence after sentence for minute details and offering honest feedback. Together we have talked through and rewritten every line and paragraph countless times to bring these events and this story to life.

Theresa Wright, thank you for inviting me into your life to meet you and your grandchildren and for allowing me to become "family," as well as for sharing private memories of your brother Paul and his letters.

Thank you to Alexis Uhl Kovacs, my talented daughter who continually encouraged me to forge ahead and not give up on the idea of this book, for helping to layout photos and using your extraordinary talents to design the book cover.

To my family members and many friends who took time to read chapters and listen tirelessly as I described and recounted scenes and ideas, thank you. And special thanks go out to our wonderful grandchildren and most enthusiastic supporters who never doubted that Grandpa's book would be published.

To my nephew, Kim Tyson, who, with the help of friends, volunteered to locate Sgt. Bill Wright, and to Bill, who willingly recounted the events of Operation Prairie, which helped pull together much-needed details that shed light on the actual occurrences of those fateful hours.

To Karen Stein, thank you for traveling this journey with us, for your professional editing and advice, and for always being there to help and answer our many questions.

To the following authors for your thoughts and suggestions: Bruce Barth, *The Martin P5M Marlin*; Nick A. Veronico, *21st-Century U.S Air Power*; John Ketwig, *. . . And a Hard Rain Fell*; Richard Thuss, *What Time Is It?*; and Joe Walpole, "We Were Here" (*ANGI Magazine*).

To Nick Veronico for connecting me with Globe Pequot Publishing Group. And many thanks to our editor David Reisch and his team at Globe Pequot. I'm deeply grateful for your belief that my story is worth telling.

NOTES

CHAPTER 1: FLASHBACK
1. Operations and Unit Maintenance Manual for Land Mines, TM-9-1345-203-12, October 1995, Department of the Army, Headquarters, Washington, DC, May 26, 2016, accessed May 14, 2020, https://www.liberatedmanuals.com/tm-9-1345-203-12.pdf.

CHAPTER 3: CHROME DOME
1. Arlington National Cemetery, https://www.arlingtoncemetery.mil.
2. JFK Presidential Library and Museum, Washington, DC, January 20, 1961, https://www.jfkLibrary.org.

CHAPTER 4: WEEKEND WARRIOR
1. *Encyclopedia Britannica*, "San Juan," August 1, 2016, accessed July 20, 2022, https://www.britannica.com/place/san-juan-puero-rico.
2. *Encyclopedia Britannica*, "Culebra Island," April 6, 2009, accessed May 1, 2020, https://www.Britannica.com/place/culebra-island.
3. *Encyclopedia Britannica*, "Vieques Island," Contrib. Amy Tikkanen, January 10, 2019, accessed April 27, 2020, https://www.britannica.com/place/vieques-island.

CHAPTER 5: "GUERRA DE ABRIL" (DOMINICAN CIVIL WAR)
1. *Encyclopedia Britannica*, "Santo Domingo," Contrib. Amy Tikkanen, February 27, 2019, accessed May 1, 2020, https://www.britannica.com/place/santo-domingo.
2. *Encyclopedia Britannica*, "Dominican Republic," Contrib. Nancie L. Gonzalez and Howard J. Wiarda, December 6, 2009, accessed May 1, 2020, https://www.Britannica.com/place/dominican-republic.

CHAPTER 6: CURAÇAO

1. *Encyclopedia Britannica*, "Willemstad," accessed May 13, 2020, https://www.Britannica.com/place/dominican-republic.

2. *Encyclopedia Britannica*, "Field Artillery," by Ian Vernon Hogg, December 31, 2014, accessed December 7, 2022, https://www.britannica.com/field-artillery.

CHAPTER 7: CALL TO DUTY

1. Anthony P. Doran, Gary Hoyt, and Charles A. Morgan III, "Survival, Evasion, Resistance, and Escape (SERE) Training: Preparing Military Members for the Demands of Captivity," chapter 11 in *Military Psychology: Clinical and Operational Applications*, ed. Carrie H. Kennedy and Eric A. Zillmer (New York: Guilford Press, 2006), 242–61, accessed April 28, 2025, https://www.ptsd.va.gov/professional/articles/article-pdf/id80573.pdf.

CHAPTER 8: DEAD RATS

1. Peter Brush, "South Vietnam's Buddhist Crisis," *Vietnam Magazine*, 2005, ©2020 HistoryNet, accessed May 2020, https://www.historynet.com/the-1966-buddhist-crisis-in-south-vietnam.

2. Peter Brush, "South Vietnam's Buddhist Crisis," *Vietnam Magazine*, 2005, ©2020 HistoryNet, accessed May 2020, https://www.historynet.com/the-1966-buddhist-crisis-in-south-vietnam.

CHAPTER 9: CHUCKLES

1. Douglas Sterner, "Jimmie E. Howard USMC," 1999, ©2019 Home of Heroes.com, accessed June 21, 2016, https://homeofheroes.com/heroes-stories/vietnam-war/jimmie-e-howard.

2. *Encyclopedia Britannica*, "Betel," August 30, 2013, accessed April 13, 2020, https://www.Britannica.com/plant/Betel.

CHAPTER 10: SUDDEN DEATH

1. Vietnam Helicopter Pilots Association (VHPA), "Helicopter Valley," webmaster Gary Roush, October 14, 2014, ©1998–2021 Vietnam Helicopter Pilots Association, accessed June 9, 2016, https://www.vhpa.org/KIA/panel/battle/66071501.HTM.

CHAPTER 11: OPERATION PRAIRIE

1. "Operation Prairie and the DMZ," MarZone.com, webmaster Victor Vilionis, ©1996–2020, accessed July 6, 2016, http://marzone.com/7thMarines/Hst0202.htm.

CHAPTER 12: SUZUKI

1. "Engineers with M16 Land Mine," Vietnamwar.govet.nz, webmaster Gareth Phipps, February 3, 2011, © Crown, accessed June 26, 2016, https://www.vietnamwar.govt.nz/photo/engineers-m16-land-mine.

2. "1975 Operation Baby Lift and Frequent Wind," Air Force Historical Support Division, Capt. Gregory Ball, November 1989, accessed December 30, 2022, http://www.afhistory.af.mil/FAQs/Fact-Sheets/Article/458955/1975-operation-babylift-and-frequent-wind.

CHAPTER 13: SHORT-TIMERS

1. *Encyclopedia Britannica*, "Sila," accessed April 28, 2025, https://www.britannica.com/topic/sila-Buddhism.

2. "Combined Action Program History," USMC CAC Oscar, webmaster F. J. Taylor, accessed June 8, 2014, https://sites.google.com/site/usmccaposcar/cap-history?authuser=0.

CHAPTER 14: NO PLACE LIKE HOME

1. Martin Luther King Jr., "Beyond Vietnam: A Time to Break the Silence" (speech delivered at Riverside Church, New York City, April 4, 1967), https://www.commondreams.org/views/2018/01/15/beyond-vietnam-time-break-silence.

CHAPTER 15: LIFE GOES ON

1. Clare Harner, *The Gypsy*, 1938.

www.ingramcontent.com/pod-product-compliance
Lightning Source LLC
Chambersburg PA
CBHW021956090426
42811CB00001B/50